Contents

Dedication

To Angelika

WORDS and IMAGES on the PAGE

improving children's writing through design

14

WITHDRAWN

Paul Johnson

WITHDRAWN

David Fulton Publishers
London

185 346 4430

David Fulton Publishers Ltd
2 Barbon Close, London WClN 3JX

First published in Great Britain by David Fulton Publishers 1996

Note: The right of Paul Johnson to be identified as the author of this work has been asserted by him in accordance with the Copyright, Designs and Patents Act 1988.

Copyright © Paul Johnson

British Library Cataloguing in Publication Data

A catalogue record for this book is available from the British Library

ISBN 1-85346-443-0

Typeset by The Harrington Consultancy Ltd, London EC1B 0AP
Printed in Great Britain by Bell & Bain Ltd, Glasgow

Acknowledgements

Particular thanks are expressed to the staff and children at Beaver Road Junior and Infants School, Manchester, and Birchfields Primary School, Manchester, for allowing me total access to so many of their book art projects; also a special thanks to the staff and children of the following schools for allowing me to reproduce their pupils' work: Abingdon Primary School, Stockport; Byley County Primary School, Cheshire; Castle Hill School, Stockport; Cheadle Primary School, Stockport; Christ the King RC Primary School, Manchester; Dial Park Primary School,Stockport; Hexthorpe Primary School, Doncaster; Kelsall County Primary School, Cheshire; Mills Hill Primary School, Oldham; Norbury Hall Primary School, Stockport; Queens Road Primary School, Stockport; Reddish Vale Nursery School, Stockport; Rose Hill Primary School, Stockport; St Thomas CE Primary School, Coppice, Oldham; Victoria Road County Primary School, Northwich, Cheshire.

The Beginning of Psalm 80, 13th century, is reproduced by courtesy of the Director and University Librarian, the John Rylands Library, University of Manchester.

The illustration from *Billy's Beetle* (Mick Inkpen, 1991) is reproduced by courtesy of Mick Inkpen and Hodder Headline PLC. The illustration from *Fairy Tales* (W. Heath Robinson, 1913) is reproduced by courtesy of the estate of Mrs J. C. Robinson.

A particular thanks to my colleague, Nigel Hall, for so many valuable suggestions in the preparation of the text.

Finally, a personal thanks to my wife, Ercelia, for allowing me access to her own researches with children, and for preparing for reproduction many of the illustrations shown in this book.

Introduction

Any text or image presented uncomfortably to the eye will take longer to reach the comprehending mind and may even deter the reader from trying to understand the author's text.

John Ryder (1993)

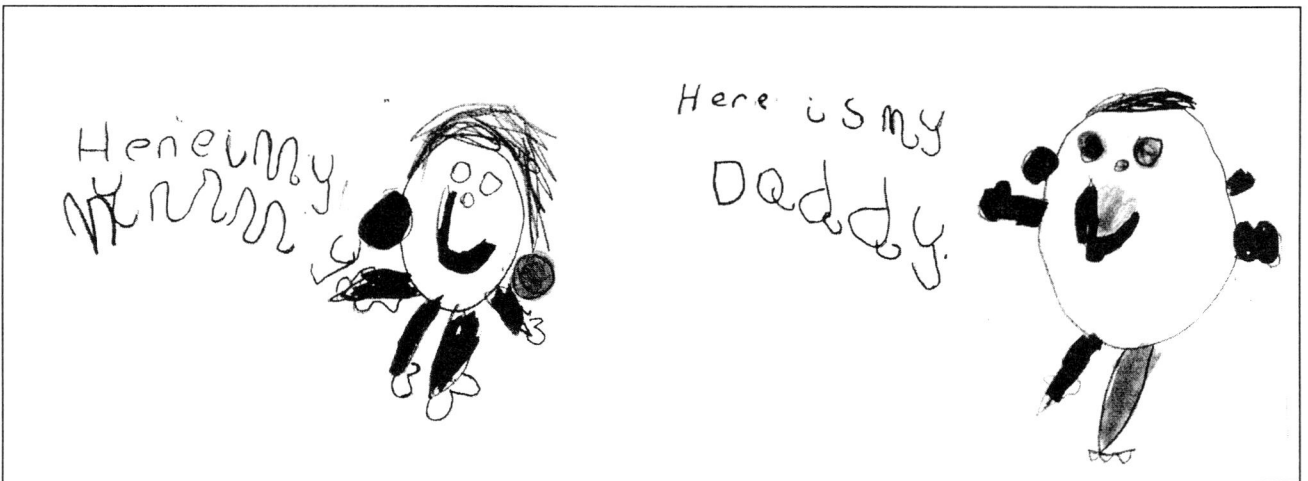

My Family Zarina
Already, at four years of age Zarina is organising words and pictures in designated locations in the book form.

Not only does good graphic design eliminate uncertainty and present information in the best possible way, it also sends out messages about the quality of the culture it comes from. Whenever children write on a piece of paper or process words on a computer, design concepts are brought into play. Professional book designers arrange words and images on the page to maximum effect, but it is so easy to overlook, when attempting to develop children's writing, that they also need 'design awareness' in order to think clearly on paper and state in the sharpest way possible what they want to say.

This book attempts to show how this can best be accomplished.

The page

Images of any kind, whether words or drawings, produced electronically or by hand, have an organic interrelationship, conditioned by the spatial arena of that magical rectangle – 'the page'.

How do we help children 'see' and manipulate this world of graphic communication? Children deadened by the inactive exercise book find the organic structure of books they make themselves invigorating and stimulating; the book form opens a door into the acquisition of writing skills that is unique. Some children are 'naturals' and seem able to plan pages intuitively. Others need coaxing into a visual awareness: they miss refinements like the spacing of words. But often it is in major issues, like planning page space, that they succumb to visual ineptitude, and this restricts the clarity of their communication. Success and failure can coexist on the same page and in several different contexts. Each piece of work is a step in a series of steps, hopefully better than what has gone before, but not as good as what is to follow. The main thrust of meaning comes from what the text interacting with the illustration 'says'. However sophisticated and stylish the design, if the content of the designed material is weak the page is a failure.

Turning over a new leaf

In this discussion of graphic design in the classroom equal status is given to both writing and illustrating, just as it is in the world of communication; but of course picture-making should always emerge organically from a need for visual expression and knowledge of when a written episode is asking to be illustrated. The parcelling of writing and illustration by design should be at the centre of the learning experience, whatever the subject area. However, this book is predominantly, although not exclusively, concerned with one of the most fundamental and popular forms of writing – the narrative. Although the primacy of the narrative genre has been questioned in some literacy circles, it is the illustrated children's story book which often first inspires the young to read, and which eventually leads them to sophisticated modes of adult reading. If children understand how illustrations coexist with text, and gain insight into the episodic nature of both forms by producing picture story books themselves, they will acquire skills not only in story writing, but 'good' writing in all its forms.

Graphic design

The Encyclopaedia of Graphic Design and Designers (Livingstone and Livingstone, 1992) describes graphic design as a 'Generic term for the activity of combining typography, illustration, photography and printing for the purposes of persuasion, information or instruction'. The term 'graphic design' sounds esoteric and abstruse, but there can be few teachers who do not use the most basic of graphic design skills when, for example, mounting children's work for display purposes. By training the eye to 'think graphically', a new world of communicating is opened, even for the youngest of children. As we shall see later, the psychology of textual space is very different from that of illustration space. What can 'work' in a rectangle of words can fail when the same space is engaged with line drawing. Combining words and pictures so that they complement each other successfully is the art of the book.

Hand-generated images

Much attention is given today to children learning to generate texts and graphics electronically, but hand-written and hand-drawn images have a special place in a child's development. Whenever I visit a professional design studio the design team always seems to be as busy with fibre-tipped pens and layout sheets as with computers. There is something uniquely dynamic about making marks directly with the hand using a variety of tools and materials; it is highly personal and intimate, and in the same way the paper book has a charm which the electronic book lacks. I think it was Degas who said that the hand was designed to hold a pencil. There is a growing number of published books that are entirely written and illustrated by hand, such as Sara Midda's *Sketchbook from Southern France* (1990) and, in another context, Robin Lawrie's visual interpretation of C.S. Lewis's

The Lion, the Witch and the Wardrobe (1993).

This book, then, addresses the forms of writing and illustration that can be produced by any number of people working together on kitchen table, classroom desk, playground bench or carpeted floor, using basic hand-held tools. Needless to say, these techniques can then be transferred to and further developed in other areas of English and art, and on the computer.

Taken to book

Throughout this book I have used children's work, not only to *illustrate* design concepts and the common mistakes that are made by the young, but also, more significantly, to *define* design concepts. Much of the work shown here is from urban schools in which teachers struggle to raise the expectations and accomplishments of average and below-average pupils. I have therefore tried to reflect the norm of what is produced in these schools, and the levels of achievement it is reasonable to expect, rather than to seek out clever or 'artistic' pupils.

'Book logic' can transform pupils' weak textual material into confidently articulated statements. In order to concentrate on writing as design, I have therefore left largely undiscussed the 'what' and 'how' of children's writing and the skills of illustration. Similarly, the social and behavioural aspects of book art projects with the young are barely touched upon. What I hope teachers will find useful is how to introduce graphic design awareness to children as they write, so that many of the frustrations the young experience in communicating often quite basic pieces of information can be overcome.

A book should be like an evolving symphony, new ideas demanding structures to convey them which are also new. When children take control of their own learning by becoming successful writers and illustrators, they experience the thrill of the professional author and the joy of communicating their ideas to others with vividness and clarity.

Chapter I

Will-be Authors

The structure of the page is a fundamental part of visual communication. Whereas the decorative and expressive aspects of the page may be understood and implemented only by the designer, the structure of the page must be understood by the writer, the typesetter, and the production artist as well, because all make decisions that directly affect the outcome of the design.

Suzanne West (1990)

Aspiring children's picture book authors and illustrators learn their craft by looking at what has gone before. They are fortunate in having in Britain some of the best and most original writers for children in the world. From 'how to-be-a-children's-author-and-illustrator' books the aspiring exponent soon learns that before undertaking writing and drawing it makes sense to know what a children's picture book is *from a design point of view*. Thus, the *form* the book will take can be determined during the early stages of conceiving an *idea* for it – one has a strategic influence on the other. This is an excellent starting point for children to improve their own writing – so how does one learn how story books are created? Bicknell and Trotman, in their guide to the would-be professional children's author (1988), classify picture book layout designs. The principal page-spread designs they identify are:

- Formal
- Balanced formal
- Free style
- Few key words dominated by illustration
- Illustration with text below
- Picture 'spots' dropped into story blocks
- Window of text in full double-page illustration.

Formal

Left page writing, right page illustration is the classical design strategy of children's books, exemplified by Hans Christian Andersen's *Fairy Tales* (1913), illustrated by W. Heath Robinson. It is a model of good book design from the 'Golden Age' of children's picture books.

In its simplest form, a one-sentence text acts as a kind of caption for the facing illustration. This is a sound base for children planning their own narratives and helps to discourage the confused texts that so many of them produce. The pupils in Philip's class were given simple concertina books (see Appendix 1) and asked to draw the first picture of their story (right side) and then write words to 'describe' it (left side). This is the framework and content of the first four pages of Philip's book:

P1 *Who is the main person in your story and where is he or she when it begins?*

'On earth there was a man, He was called Sam.'

P2 *Now bring someone or something else into your story.*

'When he was young he found a complete dinosaur skeleton.'

Formal arrangement

Hans Christian Andersen's
Fairy Tales illustrated by
W. Heath Robinson

THE NILE FLOOD HAD RETIRED

The last Dinosaur
Philip (aged 6)

On Earth there was a man
He was called Sam.

P3 *Can you think of something frightening or exciting that can happen to both of them?*

'At night it came to life. It wrecked the homes of men and women.'

P4 *What happened next?*

'At 7.00 pm it got food. Then it went back to sleep at 5.00 am...'

Balanced formal

In the balanced formal plan the area covered by the illustration is the same as that of the text. Children enlarge or reduce the narrative page episode so that it roughly corresponds to the space allocated for it. Thus they begin to learn the skills of editing a script to a prescribed word count. During a poetry workshop Robert and Emma wrote their poem on a piece of rough paper and then practised writing it to fit the space provided.

Free style

Peter breaks with the convention of horizontal writing and 'dances' the words into a shape of their own. This is not arbitrary, but follows the shapes of the subject matter. Consequently, the beginning of the story: 'One bright sunny afternoon I was walking in the country...' spirals to symbolise radiating sunlight. On the next page, the writing rises and falls in the shape of mountains. Patterns of words which twist and turn are much favoured by advertisers because they jolt the decoding eye out of its complacency: one is prompted to reorientate either one's position or the way one holds the page. To read the beginning of Peter's story, the top of the page must be revolved, and on the next page more jerky movements are necessary to make sense of it.

'I started by drawing the outline of the mountains and the sun and then wrote the [beginning of the] story in the sun', said Peter about his work. 'When I got to the end of the sun shape I carried on writing the story in the mountain shape [beneath it]. I then filled the other shapes in with drawing.'

Few key words dominated by illustration

The only words necessary in Laura's book pages are dates. The changing images of the flower tell us all we need to know about the growth process and the dates communicate the time taken for each stage of development. This plan is well suited to a number of curriculum areas, including the sciences, which use captioned graphic imagery extensively.

Balanced formal arrangement

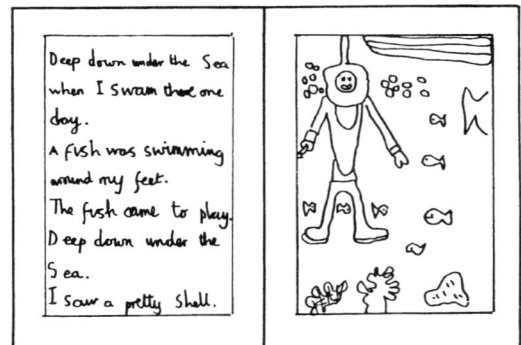

Mermaids and Daffodils
Robert and Emma (aged 6)

Free style arrangement

Few key words dominated by
illustration arrangement

One Bright Sunny Afternoon Peter (aged 10)

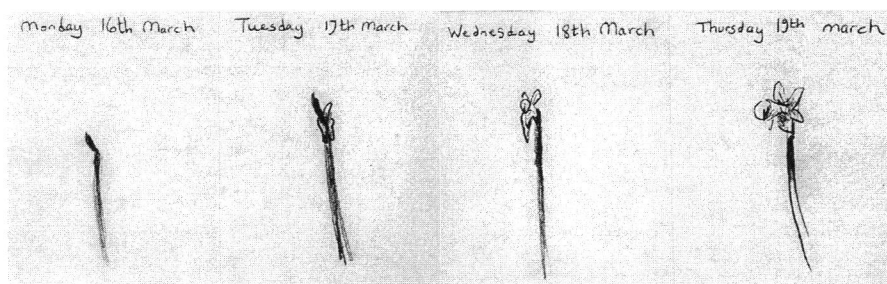

*A Week in the Life
of a Daffodil*
Laura (aged 7)

Illustration with text below

Maeve's class studied folk stories from around the world and then the pupils chose a favourite one to illustrate and rewrite in their own words. They did this in a four-page concertina book decorated with archways and made by the class teacher. The narrative was drafted and, after editing, divided into four main episodes. (Each episode continues under a flap.) Maeve said of the task: 'It started off quite easy [matching the draft to the pages] but then it got harder and I had to change the ending quite a lot. But it was good fun!'

Picture 'spots' dropped into story blocks

Amanda wrote her drafted narrative directly into an extended concertina book (see Appendix 1), pausing at interesting points to draw mini-illustrations. When she continued writing, the words had to be designed around the adjacent picture. This presents children with a 'stopping-off' visual distraction from the writing task, and makes the page setting visually exciting both for the author and the audience of younger children for which it was created.

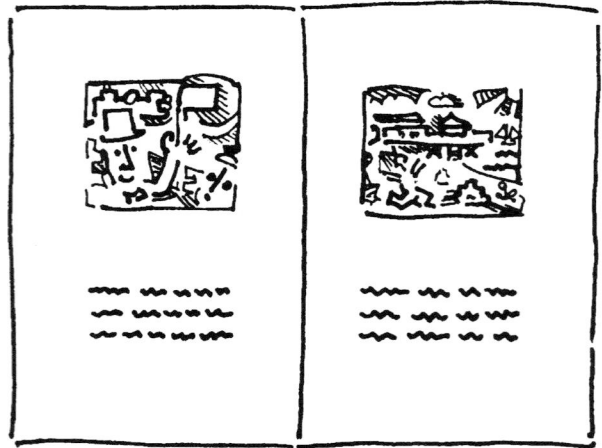

Illustration with text below arrangement

▼ *Meo!* Maeve (aged 9) ▶

Meo was a small Ethiopian boy. He was very poor. Like most families Meo's family never had enough food. Meo never saw happy, smiling faces. It was like a world of robots, one non-expressioned face after another. Meo had heard of a land far, far away where everyone smiled.

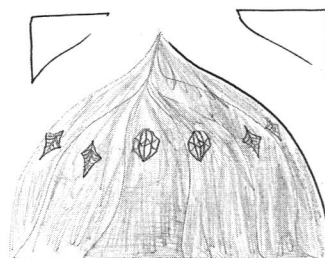

Meo knew of a place in India where a very important person lived. Everyone said it's floors were made of jewels. Meo wished he could travel far across the ocean to this palace. One day Meo and his father made a small rowing boat out of tree wood. Meo loved his boat. Every day Meo took his boat to the nearly dry river.

Picture 'spots' dropped into story blocks arrangement

Chapter 2
What Happened Next?

As I was running along, I Ux looked up. There, above me was a building rocking. "Ohno." I cried. The buildings rocks were falling upon me. Then, within seconds, the whole building fell on top of me. I tried to scream but my mouth filled with rocks and stones. I lay there, all alone. I was thinking that a horrible creature was about to kreep creep out of the soil and bash me up. The things above me seemed to be jumping up and down. Well, thats what it sounded like. The shaking and trembling up above was still going on. My left leg seemed

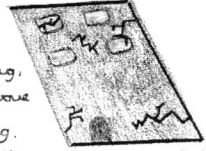

The Earthquake Amanda (aged 9)

It took Leo a long time. He ate only a little food. He slept only 2 hours a day, maybe less. It taken him 6 weeks to get only half way. Now he was into his 12th week. He had stopped 3 times, 5 days each stop and collected food and water. Finally he got there. India. He got out of his boat and hid it behind a rock. Then he set on foot for the Taj Mahal.

The gasards were friendly to Leo as he was so poor. The king adored Leo as he had no children of his own. He was sad when he knew Leo must go home. Leo wished his parents were here. Now he was dressed in fancy clothes. He asked the king if his parents could come. The King ordered for Leo's parents to be flown in by plane, fare payed for by himself. The man whom Leo met on the way also wanted Leo to be happy. He agreed to meet his parents at the airport.

Window of text in full double-page illustration
Pictures that reach the edges of the page ('bled' illustrations) tend to come forward sharply – as do the walls in Emma's book. They can so easily look crude, but sometimes, either by design or accident, they work. This book with decorative cut-out panels and opening doors was made by the class teacher and so Emma's task was to conceive a story to fit the form. The narrative could be designed into any part of the page. This kind of project should develop from more conventional assignments (for example, formal arrangements). Children love books with engineered doors in them, as the large number of published books in this genre shows.

Words and images interacting

We are seeing that words and pictures can interact in many ways to communicate meaning. There are limitless ways of designing almost any piece of information successfully, providing the book artist understands 'the page' as a design concept.

Window of text in full double-page illustration arrangement

Once there were four children called Rebecca, Jakie, Lucy and Amy. One day they were all playing dares and Lucy dared Jakie to go in the old spooky castle on the big hill. Jakie didn't want to be called chicken so, she did go. The door was crumbling down so it was easy to get in.

The first room didn't seem so bad but then she saw a dager in the wall. It had a piece of paper on it which did say 'ENTER AT OWN RISK!' But, the words 'at own risk' were crossed out!

The next room didn't seem to bad either. It was only then she noticed somone was following her!

She then caught a glimse of sombody. But then they ran away.

It Doesn't Look Spooky! Emma (aged 11)

Children making picture books

When children make books themselves they experience ownership in a way that no other writing form can give them. There is a history of making books in the bookbinding tradition in our schools, but 'basic books', as they have come to be known, enable children of all ages to access the book form easily and stylishly.

Basic books such as concertina books are made from single sheets of paper. Six 'working' pages plus an integral cover is the commonest form, but extended basic books can be made, comprising any number of pages. While the content of these books can be created in an improvised fashion (pupils writing and illustrating without prior planning), better results generally come from the teacher and pupil prescribing the form in advance. Andreas designed his own book as alternating text and illustration. Page 8 is reserved for 'back page copy' and the last page is the cover in the conventional format of top – title, middle – artwork, bottom – author's name. He has designed the three spreads as:

1 definition of protagonist (toucan) in setting (rain forest);
2 toucan goes on an underwater adventure;
3 toucan discovers magic gold which prevents the destruction of the rain forest.

The version reproduced here is a photocopy of the original with coloured-in illustrations. Thus several colouring techniques can be explored while the original remains intact. (Appendix 1 discusses outline structures and working strategies for these basic book forms, including the origami book.)

Lyndsay was helped as she conceived her story one page at a time in her concertina book. She had to think in a six-episode way and, as both prescribed text and illustration areas are reduced to half-page areas,

refinement is called for; only essentials can be expressed. The rhythmic arrangement of the first four pages is alternating words/illustration. Thus the picture proceeds from the text on the first page but precedes it on the second. Whereas the text on the second page flows uninterrupted to the next page-spread – one reads it as a continuation – each follow-on illustration has to be analysed as a separate visual episode. The interaction of the two decoding systems, then, is conditioned by design elements. The structural outline of her narrative (which progressed through several drafts written directly into the book, erased and rewritten as necessary) is as follows:

1 Problem: John (main character) sells out of ice cream.
2 Shared problem: seagull (supporting character) enters dialogue with John.
3 Attempted resolution: seagull and John join forces in attempt to find ice cream.
4 Complication: ice cream factory has none left.
5 Solution: seagull has ice cream recipe.
6 Resolution: John sells ice cream again.

(This book is published in *Book Box* by The Children's Press, The Book Art Project, 1994.)

Super Speed Simon ▶
Andreas (aged 7)
Alternating text and
illustration pages

John the refreshment man sold out of ice creams just as everybody wanted them.

"Hello there, what is the matter?" said the Seagull. "I have sold out of ice cream," said John.

" said, Let e take you the ice ream Factory"

When they got there they found that there was no ice cream

The Seagull said "But I've got a recipe for ice cream" So they made some.

So John was able to sell ice cream once more.

My name is Lyndsay Faraji. I am 7 years old. My hobby is Drawing.

Lyndsay Faraji is a pupil at Beaver Road Infant School, Manchester.

© Lyndsay Faraji 1994
The Book Art Project
The Manchester Metropolitan University M20 2RR

The Children's Press

The Book Art Project

JOHN THE ICE CREAM MAN

LYNDSAY FARAJI

In the Amazon rain forest there are lots of animals and creatures. There is a toucan in the rain forest whose name is Super Speed Simon because he flies so fast through the air.

Simon found a remote control diving suit. Simon got in the swim suit and went in to the deep depths of the sea. He saw a shipwreck and found a map.

It led him to the temple of doom where the gold was held. He got the gold and took the gold back with him. Because the gold was magic it stopped the rain forest being

cut down. Whenever an axe was being used it turned to dust.

Andreas is 7 years old. His hobby is singing, football and making magic tricks.

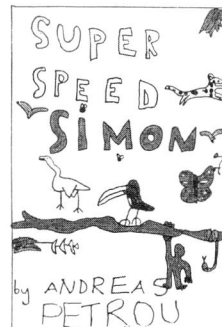

SUPER SPEED SIMON

by ANDREAS PETROU

Designing pictures

Both Andreas and Lyndsay have used their visual intelligence to make the narrative subject matter fit the prescribed space. In *Billy's Beetle* (1991) Mick Inkpen is inventive in drawing figures to fit either a whole or half page area without any sense that they have been cut down to fit the page. In one place, a man and a polar bear fill the page. On the next page, the writing at the top reduces the illustration beneath it to a half page space. To avoid diminishing the man and the polar bear in size, Inkpen draws them bending down, looking at the man's dog wagging its tail in the bell of a tuba (see pp.18–19). This creative way of making the best use of the illustration space, while bringing variety into the book design, is repeated throughout the book. It is a kind of design awareness children need to be taught as they design their books.

Modes of design

In children's illustrated books it is common to follow on blocks of text, but rarer to process several illustrations one after the other without interaction with words. The exception to this is the picture book which relies wholly on visually communicated information, as in Raymond Briggs' *The Snowman* (1978). Illustrations in the bottom half of the page tend to make pages look heavy, whereas placed in the top half of the page they appear to be balanced with the words.

Neil's illustration seems oppressed by the weight of the text above it, whereas in Peter's outdoor scene the tree seems to extend above and beyond the limits of the page. However, to give rhythmic variety, illustrations in published books invariably appear in the lower areas of pages: there is always a conflict between opposing concepts and psychological forces in graphic design!

There is, though, graphic logic to children placing the text in the upper sections of pages. It can be difficult for them to assess how much page space is needed by a drafted narrative. Writing from the page top, the child can give over the unused space to illustration – little planning is necessary. But when writing is at the bottom of the page a precise area has to be designated for it. This can lead to the provision of too large an area, leaving an uncomfortably empty space at the foot of the page, or too small an area, resulting in words rapidly diminishing in size, running off the bottom of the page, or assigned to the next page.

While there is justification for a repetitive design strategy for each page – pupils can work to a format and an audience of younger readers can read to a pattern – alternating illustration/text makes for a livelier reading experience.

Freeing the page

As skills in constructing simple narrative episodes through the formulas already discussed are accomplished, more liberal arrangements can be encouraged. But this freedom does present problems. For example, on the first spread from her book Tamara has selected what she regards to be the highlight of this section of the story and has illustrated it at the top of the right side page. However, the text is read continuously from the left page to the right one, the eye travelling back to scrutinise the illustration on completion. On the next spread she has continued the text over to the right side page and inserted a picture after the third line of text. While this varies the visual design of the book, the illustration cuts a piece of dialogue in half and therefore breaks reading continuity. It is a minor point, but as children develop page consciousness it is the kind of thing that should increasingly concern them.

The Creation Neil (aged 9)

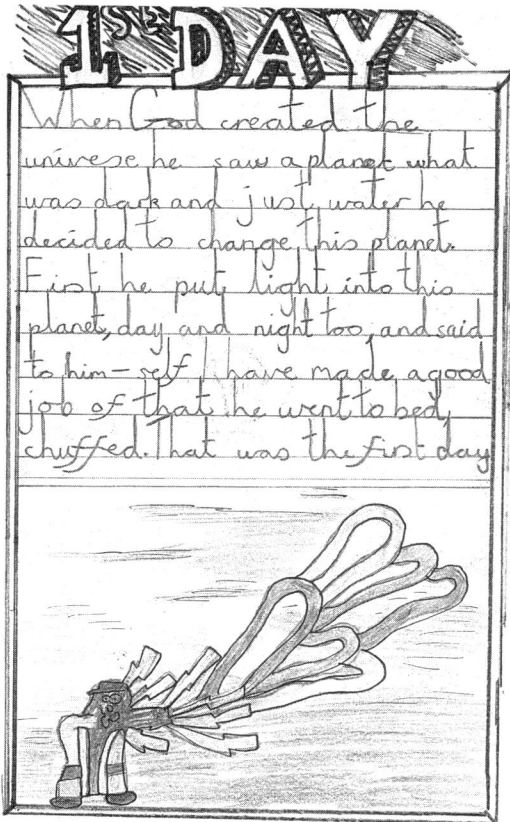

1st DAY

When God created the univrese he saw a planet what was dark and just water he decided to change this planet. First he put light into this planet, day and night too, and said to him-self I have made a good job of that he went to bed chuffed. That was the first day

The Four Seasons Peter (aged 9)

The Four Seasons

Peter Mullen

One bright day in Weather land, there lived four people called Winter, Spring, Summer, and Autumn. Winter is a cold hearted person who always bring rain and snow. On one day of the year he doesn't make it rain, he makes it snow and sometimes he uses his magic dust to make people joyful and happy. The rest of the time he makes it cold.

How the Jungle Won, Part 2 Tamara (aged 9)

14

and further into the jungle.

Bongle the hippo had now recovered from his shock and silently crept near the two men and listened to their conversation. "Oh, what's this?", he asked himself. "what's this about destroying Dinks jungle? I better go back and tell him." As he said

11

because Rodger (the bravest of the two) knocked the bewildered python on the head with a mallet.

Just as Hugie and Rodger entered the tiny

12

clearing where Bongle was snoring in his mud bog, Bongle awoke. As the hippo's head lifted a little from the mud. Hugie tripped over a fallen tree and screamed. The scream startled the poor hippo and he got up from the mud and ran into the trees. "Oh no. Rodger what was that? I feel like getting out of this

13

place immediately!" croaked Hugie but Rodger replied "of course we won't!

We are going on to destroy this Jungle! Will I have to say: Hup, two, three, four?". So off they went furter

Eve had only recently been introduced to the book arts when she made her book, but already she was selecting from a range of textual and graphic strategies to communicate the excitement of receiving Christmas presents. The first panel of this four-fold concertina book, a simple six-word prayer designed into the picture of a Christmas present, is balanced in the last panel by a longer prayer written over the torso section of a self-portrait. The two middle panels describe presents in words and pictures. Would a celebration of Christmas in essay form have been as succinct and informative as this graphic version?

A maze of strategies

A longer book than this could illustrate the many other ways in which children, through guidance, intuition or experience, have conceived and presented their ideas in the book form. Here are just a few of them:

Catherine integrates the text into the illustration area. The central illustration 'band' of *Under the Sea* provides a kind of visual interlude between paragraphs. Fitting words into an irregular shape, as in Hayley's diagonally-divided pages, is difficult because they must diminish with mathematical precision. Illustrations can be tricky too, but children love this kind of challenge. The placing of text and artwork on the page is also conditioned by subject matter. A part of Aimee's self-portrait lists her likes and dislikes and these are carefully spaced out as items arranged over the spread. Calligraphers have long played with intertwining decorative art and words. At its best, this can be an almost spiritual experience, a visual reflection on the meaning of the words that is both uplifting and inspiring. At its worst it can be a headache to decipher! How successful would you say Katie has been at integrating text with images?

Sally's Doll Catherine (aged 9)

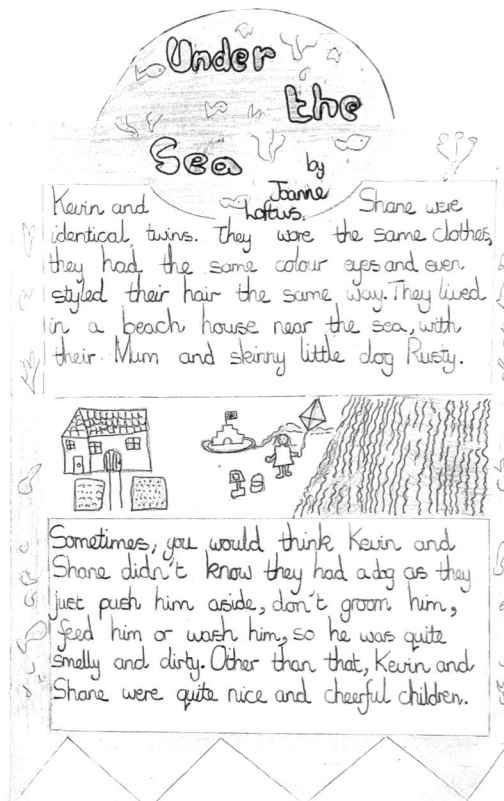

Under the Sea Joanne (aged 10)

My Christmas
Eve (aged 9)

Eve Artingstall

One of my favourite presents was a television. I was very very surprised because I didn't except it.

NEIBOUGHERS

This is a Rock n Roll Maze. It is a game and when I got it I was very pleased.

God I Thankyou for the presents I got. And I am sorry that some people got none at all. I am very lucky I got a And for getting Xata mas Prescats
Amen

Cuddly Bear
Hayley (aged 10)

cuddly bear
There was once a girl called Amy. She owned a big cuddly teddy bear. She had called it Barny. She had kept it since she had been a baby.

cuddly bear
Amy could never go to sleep without it. One day Amy's mum thought that she was too old for a teddy. So she Sold it to the school Jumble sale for 50 p.

50 p only

Me
Aimee (aged 10)

My Likes
Bananas   Swimming   Ice cream
WORD Wing   Walking
Reading   Books
Sun   Sport   Oranges   Flowers   Holidays   Music   Animals

My dislikes
Grape fruit   peppers
Nettles   rain   smelly feet
Fish   Cloth (Black)
Dogs   Throwing
School Ties   Custard   Curry   Red
Rings   T (Red)

There once lived two little children and their mother and father. They didn't have very much money. They lived in a little hut. There was a wood. At the other side of the wood was a dark cave. All they had to sleep on was some straw and hay. They had very little food! All they ate was bread and

milk. They often went through the wood. It was a very dark wood and the trees were large and the wind blew in the branches. But it was nice to hide there. The cave was even darker than the wood and they dare not go

The Two Children
Katie (aged 10)

From page to spread to complete book

Every well-designed book has a 'look', a total image. Some publishers have a house style that is inimitably their own. It is evident from the examples already presented that the page is meaningless in isolation; it has an organic relationship with the page which faces it. Some very young book artists, unable yet to make chronological relationships, will be preoccupied with the page as an entity. Through book making and contact with published illustrated books, they link the left page to the right one, and eventually to what goes on over the page. Children have so much to learn from appreciating how good children's picture books extract variation from an alternating text-picture strategy, as does Mick Inkpen's *Billy's Beetle,* already referred to.

The sniffy dog found a tuba. It belonged to a man in an oompah band.

'I don't think Billy's beetle is in there,' said the bandsman. 'But we will help you look.'

So the oompah band played and off they went again. Oompah! Oompah! Sniff, sniff, sniff!

Spread from Mick Inkpen's *Billy's Beetle*

The whole story

Two books, one by an infant and the other by a top junior, show the progress from page to spread to book.

The first example of Caitlan's work comes from her exercise book. The format is basic: the first right side page combines writing and image but thereafter they are separated – writing one side of the spread and a picture the other. Through examining picture story books with her teacher she became aware of 'the page concept' and the exercise book pages have helped her to place the parts of the story episodically. But then Caitlan is introduced to the basic concertina book. She wants to rewrite her story in it at once; it influences her structuring enormously. She starts by using the alternating text/ illustration spread format of her exercise book, but then switches to a strategy of single pages divided into illustration/text. She is finding that she can get more information on the page this way, and that it gives her greater freedom in how she communicates it – for example, the single image of the ladder and caption on page 5 which leads nicely into the reverse four pages of the book. The narrative structure runs thus:

The first spread introduces in artwork and writing the main character, Teddy, and, what is to become the central feature of the plot, his ladder.

'Once upon a time there was a Teddy called Ted. Teddy had a ladder.'

Cautious at first, Caitlan uses a page template to place the block of text but from here on she designs the pages more freely. The second spread is now divided into four parts in an illustration/text, text/illustration pattern. Almost professionally, Caitlan reduces the previous narrative to one sentence per page, so that the aerial on the house and the ladder are revealed separately both in words and pictures.

'One day Teddy looked up and saw that his television aerial was bent.'

'Teddy got his ladder.'

The final three pages of illustration/text suggest that this is a design strategy she feels serves her needs. Page 6 describes the next episode simply and directly,

'He put it next to the house and he climbed up.'

The climax of the story comes next on the penultimate page,

'Big Teds ladder had got whyls on so it slipt down with a big crash'

The illustration shows the ladder now lying on the ground with Teddy drawn in suspended animation. The final sequence is the rather sad conclusion to the story,

'Ted fell off the roof and hurt his leg.'

Not only are the illustrations more comprehensive here than in the exercise book version, but Caitlan also seems to be fully aware of how professional books work, communicating a succession of events which tell a shaped story. The class teacher who organised this project described her reaction on seeing books like Caitlan's emerge as 'thrilling'. Little help was given to Caitlan in planning the stages of the book; so much of what she wrote and drew came from her own spontaneous response to the page.

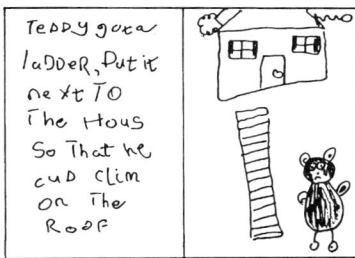

Teddy Falls off the Roof
Caitlan (aged 5)

▼ *Teddy is Gud*
Caitlan (aged 5)

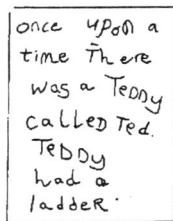

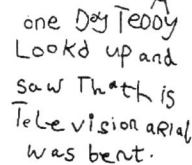

The page as art

Friends follows none of the page divisions already defined. Every page is a work of art, strung together harmoniously to make a coherent book. The narrative outline of the book's seven episodes is as follows:

Friends Joanne (aged 10)

1 There was a land far away where a group of animals lived happily together except for one, Clive the Crocodile, who was evil. Belinda Bee goes missing, although Freddy Frog was expecting to meet her at the Coconut Coffee Shop. Rachel Rabbit goes to Belinda's home in search of her.

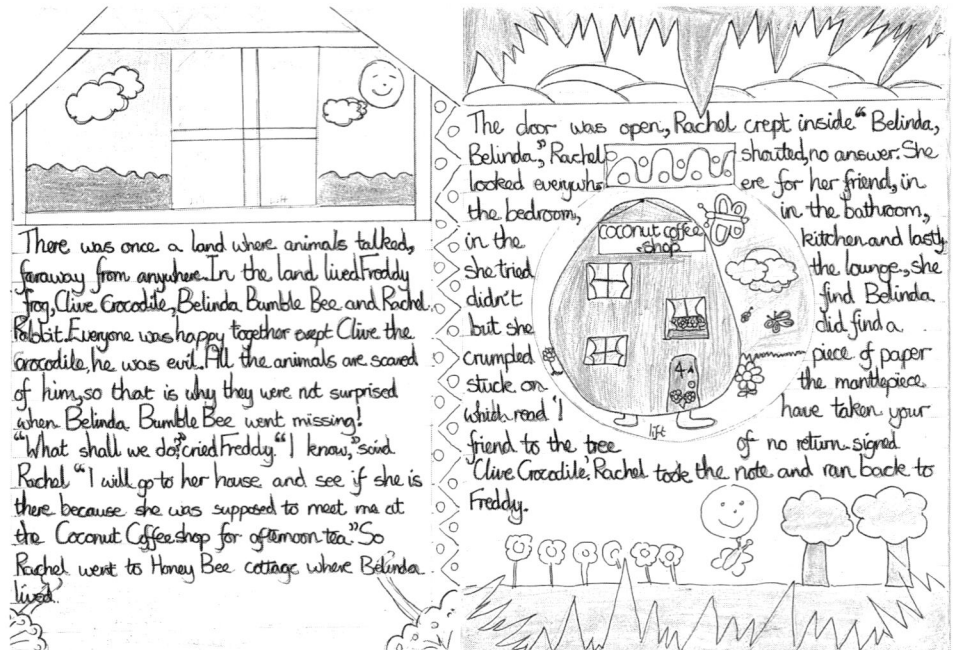

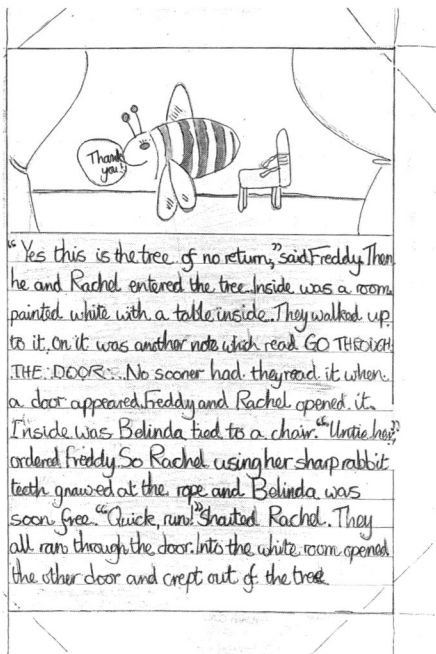

Graphic arrangement of *Friends*

2 Belinda isn't there, but a crumpled piece of paper says that she has been taken to the 'tree of no return' by Clive. Rachel runs back to Freddy.

3 Here there is a dialogue between Freddy and Rachel about the dilemma they find themselves in.

4 They decide to go to the 'tree of no return', despite the risks, and set up camp by it, waiting for dawn. The next morning they enter the tree by a secret door in its side.

5 Inside, finding Belinda tied to a chair, they set her free.

"Thats it! We'll have to look for her," he said. "We can't go there," said Rachel. "We may never come back." "She's our friend we must," said Freddy. "Yes you're right, we must," said Rachel.

So that evening, Rachel and Freddy, with their rucsacks on their backs set off for the tree of no return. They arrived at half past eight. They put up their tents, Freddy set his alarm clock for 5 o'clock in the morning, then they both went to sleep. Bring Bring, Freddy's clock had gone off at exactly 5 o'clock. "Up we get," said Rachel. Freddy and Rachel got up very quietly and got dressed. They then ran their hands up the tree trunk until they found a bump. Rachel pushed very hard against the bump and a little door opened in the tree..

FRIENDS

Rachel and Belinda came out from hiding and the three friends made Clive crocodile promise he would change and become a nice crocodile. Then from then on everyone was friends together. THE END

FRIENDS

by Joanne

To Rachel

6 As they leave the tree Clive appears, but Freddy snaps a twig off the tree and props Clive's mouth open with it.

7 Belinda, Rachel and Freddy make Clive promise to be a nice crocodile in future, and they all become friends.

The decorative style and illustration manner of each page is different. On the first page the top quarter illustration shows, beneath a flap, the land where the animals live. There are vertical decorative borders here but only top and bottom imagic borders to the second page. Here, the circular central illustration depicting the Coconut Coffee Shop is on a flap which lifts to reveal the shop interior. The third page is predominantly illustration and has rather voluptuous border decorations which are frames within frames. It pictures Belinda's house, with a rabbit flap for Rachel Rabbit, under a night sky of stars and the crescent moon. The next page has a conical design which holds the penned narrative. This creates two triangular outer panels which contain illustrations: a night scene showing Freddy and Rachel's tents and the alarm clock set to go off at five am; and a daytime picture of the 'tree of no return'. The first page on the other side of the concertina book is mainly text, but an area at the top designed like a stage portrays the released Belinda with a balloon 'Thank you' coming from her mouth. The penultimate textual page places the text slightly above half way, with a small, well-balanced illustration to top and a larger one to bottom. At the top is the scene around the tree with, beneath it, Clive the crocodile, the twig wedged in his mouth. (The 'laws' of visual perception mean that the eye gives more emphasis to the top illustration than to the bottom one: thus the one above can be smaller yet have the same 'weight' as the one below.) The final page is a visual celebration of the four characters with the closing narrative in the lower area. Again, a border frame has been

placed inside an outer one. The cover design is a rich amalgamation of title lettering and drawings of the characters 'portrayed within', in a dominant diamond shape with decorative borders. The excessive embellishment of the first side of the book is relieved by simpler decorative structures on the other side. Perhaps Joanne has learnt by experience that you can have too much of a good thing and that prodigious ornament can sometimes make text and pictures harder to decipher.

The book as theatre

Like so many books written for and by children, this book behaves like theatre, almost a melodrama, with stage sets and a 'goodies and baddies' plot. The actors enter and exit on cue and the well lit props, scenery and backcloths provide a magical setting. Each page is a wholly new visual experience, inventiveness boldly and confidently displaying itself. For all its clichéd images, both in writing and illustration technique, it imaginatively fits the prescribed form. A sheet of paper simply folded into panels has made this piece of work possible. In conversation with Joanne about how she conceived the book, she described how, although she had an outline of the story firmly established, most of the unfolding of the plot was done one page at a time. As she approached a new page, a rough outline was planned for artwork and decoration, and the narrative developed into this organised design.

This was not Joanne's first book, for she had already served a book art 'apprenticeship', developing and improving her style gradually. Her teacher had arranged book design workshops for the whole class over a period of time and many of the design issues discussed in these chapters had been worked through. Art alone could not have stimulated the continuum of pictorial, decorative and design elements celebrated in *Friends* without the cardinal influence of the penned narrative. Conversely, the text would have been less inventive without picture-making adding so many ideas to it. The narrative plot, as a verbal creation (Joanne's words were 'I *told* myself the story'), has fed her imagination with these visual images which have been realised in both pictures and illustrative border images. Nearly every page selects more than one incident from the plot and illuminates it in a uniquely visual way, in the tradition of medieval book artists, late nineteenth-century book designers and the best of children's book creators today.

Children working on their books

Chapter 2

The Ageless Page

Many children never learn how to use the conventions developed for books over the last thousand years...Many of these things can be discussed with children when they are reading with you, but they can also be introduced into the books children make for themselves. Book-making is a really useful way to introduce children to the conventions of books and to the kinds of decisions that designers have to make in producing the books they read.

Sue Walker (1992)

The traditional concepts of what constitutes a well designed page are of immeasurable importance to children in the planning of their own writing. They are based on the principles of Greek mathematics and geometry, rediscovered during the Renaissance, and although book designers have reacted against them, particularly in this century, they still hold good in publishing today.

The design inheritance

Christopher de Hamel (1992) has been particularly instrumental in uncovering the design awareness that went into every part of the great illuminated manuscripts of the late medieval period. At the end of the nineteenth century William Morris, at his Kelmscott Press, revitalised this notion of visual refinement in book design and set a standard for twentieth century publishers.

In *The Form of the Book* (1992) the revered typographer, Jan Tschichold, identified precise compositional rules for books, like

the formal structure of their preliminary matter – half title, frontispiece, title page, imprint, dedication, preface, contents, introduction (or foreword), all with traditional left or right page designations – and rules about the standard number of lines to the page, the degree of letter spacing, and its optical correctness in relation to word spacing.

The visionary teacher and artist, Robin Tanner, guided by the genius of Morris, revealed the pristine simplicity which lay beneath classical principles of book design and children's grasp of it. In *Lettering for Children* (1946) he examined individual pieces of children's work with a critical eye, stating, in one case, that in a book where the pupil had drawn large margins it would have been better to have used smaller handwriting. Looking at this example, one can see immediately what he means, but

A Note by William Morris on his aims in founding the Kelmscott Press
William Morris (1898)

▶

NOTE BY WILLIAM MORRIS ON HIS AIMS IN FOUNDING THE KELMSCOTT PRESS.❧ ❧

I BEGAN printing books with the hope of producing some which would have a definite claim to beauty, while at the same time they should be easy to read and should not dazzle the eye, or trouble the intellect of the reader by eccentricity of form in the letters. I have always been a great admirer of the calligraphy of the Middle Ages, & of the earlier printing which took its place. As to the fifteenth-century books, I had noticed that they were always beautiful by force of the mere typography, even without the added ornament, with which many of them are so lavishly supplied. And it was the essence of my undertaking to produce books which it would be a pleasure to look upon as pieces of printing and arrangement of type. Looking at my adventure from this point of view then, I found I had to consider chiefly the following things: the paper, the form of the type, the relative spacing of the letters, the words, and the while most of us can sense when a page of beautiful lettering does not fall comfortably on the eye, it takes a practised eye to spot the cause of the problem.

Critically observed pages

One can learn to look critically at a page of writing and artwork, and undertake what John Ryder (1993) calls 'visual editing'. As teachers are only too aware, children can be over-critical of their work and may discard hours of effort because one small part of a drawing or diagram fails to please. If they start with some very basic approaches to their book-oriented graphic work, many common problems can be overcome.

Learning from the professionals

The best of children's picture and information books should be used as a guide to good design. In these days of starved school and public library resources, new books are increasingly hard to come by. Not all of them, admittedly, are exemplars of excellence. The best have original and well-written stories, often reflecting the socio-political issues and concerns of the times with exquisite illustrations which probe the thinking eye of the reader through being skilfully designed and visually challenging. Other books are good in parts, and a few are good for nothing. As teachers, we must learn to be selective and critical. An unoriginal and dull narrative, despite having appetising pictures, fails. A book, excellently designed and ideal for illustrating a book-making project, may be rejected because of timid narrative and stereotypical pictures. It may take a search to find the book which meets all the criteria for the scheme you have in mind.

Variety in unity

A typical picture book may start with left page text, right page illustration, followed by two pages of alternating half-page text/illustration, followed by full double-page spread illustration. Next can come a strip cartoon-style page, divided into six boxes, with a facing page given over to one enormous word, and then back to half-page text/illustration, and so on. When the author is the illustrator (or works closely with the illustrator) the entire book can be constructed holistically. It is from this working methodology that children learn to shape their own texts within a graphically-conceived framework.

The page grid

Designing the page arrangements of text-only books is basically a matter of determining page dimensions, typeface, point size and width of margins. If, as in most children's books today, the design is much more complex than that – pages containing varying blocks of text and illustrations – laying out the page is no simple process. To bring order and cohesion to this design complexity, pages are divided into spatial zones to which the text and artwork relate – the grid. The graphic designer, Alan Swann (1989), sees a well-planned grid as an essential building block for any design on paper. Learning how to apply it can give page designs unity and vitality.

Most children, with assistance, can learn to line up the edge of a block of text with that of an illustration, thus giving basic uniformity to the page. Some, as we have seen, will venture beyond this formative design awareness and plan their books systematically. However, it is worth examining the grid idea further, because some of the problems that pupils experience in presenting their work can be solved through it.

Examples of layout preparations

Single column grids

The single column arrangement is the traditional grid for portrait-oriented books. The foot is twice the depth of the head, the fore-edge is twice the width of the gutter, the gutter is three-quarters the size of the head. While less visually satisfying, wide centrefold margins enable easy reading and comfortable holding. (Wide outer margins are known as 'scholars' margins' because historically they provided space for the reader to make notes.) There are many variations of single and double column margin widths, each for different purposes and uses. Some very wide gutter and fore-edge margins, called 'luxury margins' for obvious reasons, grace those books where economy is not a consideration.

The thinking eye

Their are many strategies for pupils producing their own books. Younger children often work directly into them, while those at a later stage plan a text with regard to the known page dimensions, draft and edit it, and then transfer the material into presentation form. A badly designed page of words and artwork glares at you. If, for example, the caption under an illustration does not line up with it, or a page heading almost disappears off the right side of the paper, one's visual antennae flinch, bruised by the aesthetic insensitivity. But it can be one thing to sense poor design and another knowing how to correct it.

What is good design?

This raises the question of what is meant by 'good design'. It cannot be reduced simply to rules of visual grammar. What some would see as 'bad design' is, in some progressive practices today, seen as 'good design'. But those initiating themselves into the clarity of vision that book art offers need guidelines. Experience will enable you to have your own ideas about defining 'good design' and to make critical judgments about what it is, or should be.

Elements of page design

Suzanne West (1990) categorises the elements of page design as:

- typographic – title, text, captions, page numbers.
- graphic – enhancement of typography, lines around text and other non-pictorial elements.
- illustration – artwork, diagrams, photo-graphs, charts.
- decoration – that which is neither necessary or useful, but which adds visual interest.

If one replaces the word 'typography' with the word 'handwriting', these four groupings are relevant to the way children construct their own texts within a visual framework. They provide an infrastructure for assessing pupils' endeavours when they write and draw images on the page.

Say precisely what you mean to say

Nicole breaks all the rules about good book design. There are no borders and both the artwork and the text cross the centrefold, yet am I alone in finding this book a very satisfying visual experience? In an inexplicable way, and as in so many young children's work, the parts seem to hold together. Alas, with older pupils it doesn't always seem to work quite like that.

Defining the proportions of the page spread

▶

Mummy and Daddy
Nicole (aged 4)

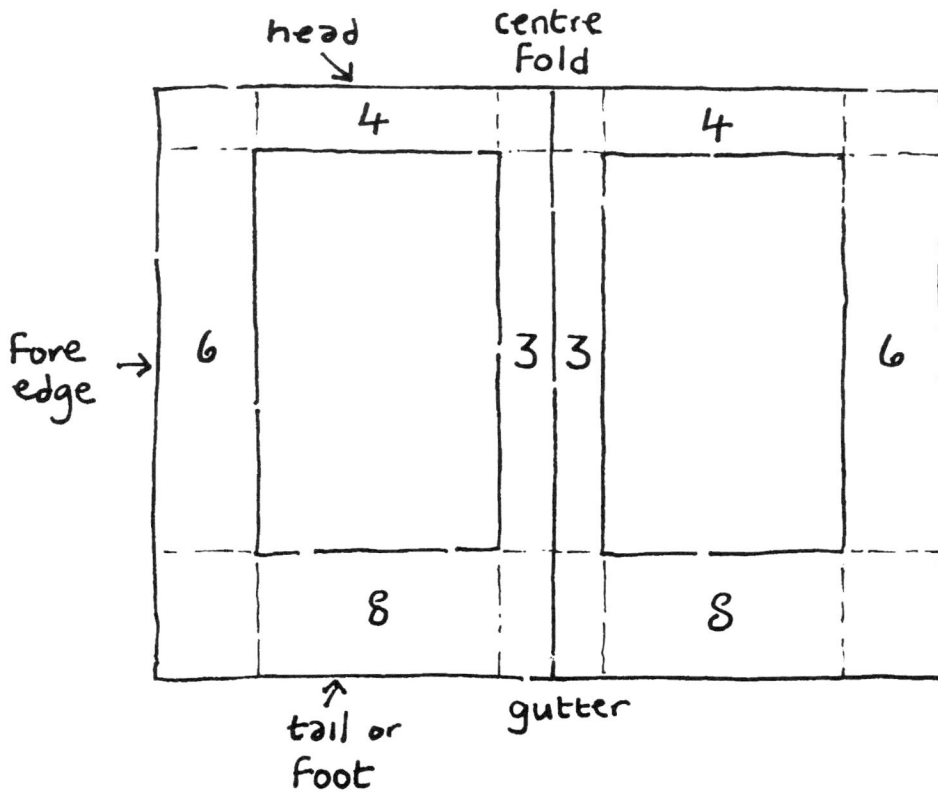

head

centre
Fold

| | 4 | | | 4 | |

fore
edge →

6 | 3 | 3 | | 6

8 | | S

tail or
foot

gutter

Beginners' problems

Michael was given a small, six-page, origami book and asked if he would write a story about Father Christmas directly into it. It was suggested that he might like to put an illustration on each page. The first page, headed 'Down the Chimney', leads off with an illustration and the remainder of the page is committed to text. Although Michael has a preconceived plot he is writing blind here. He has given no thought to the page as an object with defined edges. By the third line he is beginning to sense that the page will not go on for ever and, in that realisation, his writing begins to shrink. Five lines on he is aware that the bottom of the page is approaching perilously fast, and so the lines draw even closer together. With what must have been a sigh of relief, he discovers that he can complete the first part of the narrative, with room to spare, before crashing out of the page. In 'Chapter 2', Michael, chastened by the experience of the previous page, is now wary of running out of space and has approximated the area needed for the text. He has estimated this well, but the illustration, starting unnecessarily low on the page, has crushed the text too far down so that it sits, precariously, on the page's tailpiece. By the next page, 'Chapter 3', the illustration has been raised and occupies a smaller area than before, providing a comfortable space beneath for a fairly well proportioned block of writing.

Although Michael has been guided by his teacher, much has been learnt empirically. Each new page design is an intelligent improvement on its predecessor. If this story had been written in an exercise book none of these spatial concepts would have been encountered. What the book form brings to the reader's attention is how words communicate visually. A developing sensitivity to the book concept has led Michael to see that each page should contain a new part of his story. He rambles on at first, not thinking too much about how the words will appear on the page, but that changes. With hindsight and guidance it would not have taken much effort for him to have reduced the first part of the narrative to the same length as the other pages without any loss of meaning, indeed with sharper story-line clarity. Only the hidden organic structure of the page could make that qualitative observation possible.

Isolating page space

Sarah's story was written in an exercise book. After editing by the teacher, she was given a concertina book to transfer it into. 'Normally,' said her teacher, 'I wouldn't dream of expecting children like Sarah to, in a sense, draft a narrative, but the book form is such a fantastic thing to work in that she, and the other children in the class, did not see this transfer as drudgery and were more than willing to do it.' The book form was discussed and each page was identified as holding a part of the story, just like the books Sarah read herself. Metaphorically, the book had now been visited and touched and scented. When Sarah started writing in the book it had been defined for her as a kind of house – every page being a different room and every room having a different use. Once these preliminaries were completed, and with help from the class teacher, she subdivided the narrative into four main sections, each with its own illustration and page design. This book was a landmark in Sarah's literacy development.

My Christmas Book Michael (aged 7)

The Naughty Baby Sarah (aged 6)
(exercise book)

The Naughty Baby
(transfer from exercise book to basic book)

Planning in frames

Lisa has thought about her border designs, for she has used the page's theme as the repetitive motif – Squirrel, page l; bus stop, page 3; shopping basket, page 4. This wide frame to the text/illustration space sets off the area even more than in Sarah's book above. Accentuated focus on the textual area sharpens the child's perception not only to *what* should go inside it, but also *why.* (Borders are discussed in greater detail in the next chapter.)

Storyboards

The storyboard enables children, particularly younger ones, to plan and sequence their stories because they see the narrative box by box as it grows. There are only a few months between the two pieces of Zadir's work. English is his second language, and so the book form has provided a framework for him to handle a new language.

Squirrel Goes Shopping Lisa (aged 6)

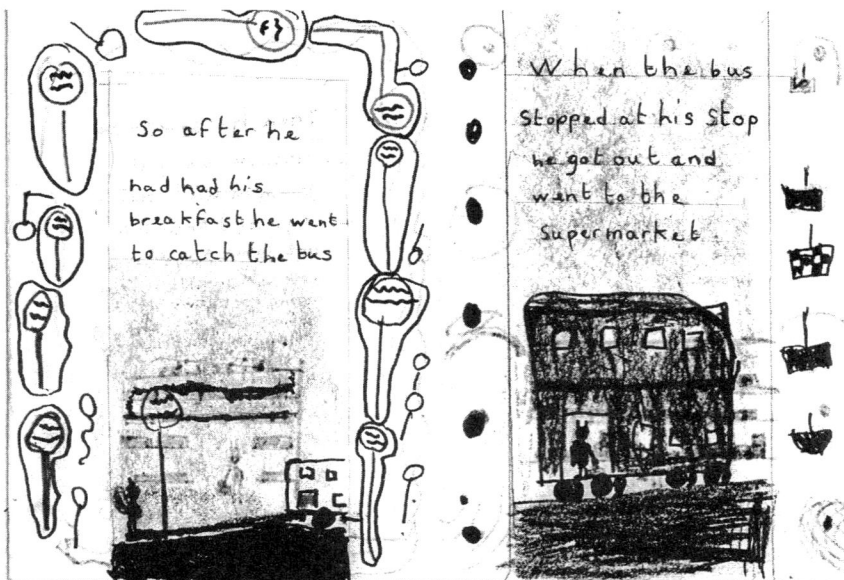

The Troll (storyboard) Zadir (aged 7)

I was out Walking with
A friend in the park
when suddenly a huge
Hole appeared in front
of us.

In the hole there was a
man. The man got
up and Sat on the
round about.

The Man in the Hole Zadir

Movable texts

Texts written on pieces of paper can be trimmed to size and then laid on the book page to find the best position for them. The print-out of a word-processed text has been pasted on to the least interesting part of the book page in *Gold Block*.

In *My Diary* the class were given the task of writing and drawing about themselves in school, on separate pieces of paper. These were trimmed down, mounted by the teacher, and presented in a book.

Natalie's book is designed like a photograph album. The illustrations are slotted into corner mounts cut on the diagonal. Children feel more relaxed about making illustrations if they are detached from the book form. Several attempts can be made, if need be, before a satisfactory picture is selected.

Lost in Space is a group book made by pupils with special educational needs. They took it in turn to word process a story they had constructed as a group, and illustrated it individually. The book was assembled by a member of staff and the pages laminated with a protective acetate covering. The book, with several others like it, became a focus of attention in the school library, and did much to raise the confidence of those engaged on it.

One day Ian asked his dad if he could go to Foge's house to play. His dad replied "yes" without glanceing up from his paper. Ian went out and got on his skate board, and wizzed out of the gate.

Gold Block
Billy and Matthew
(aged 10)

My Diary John (aged 5)

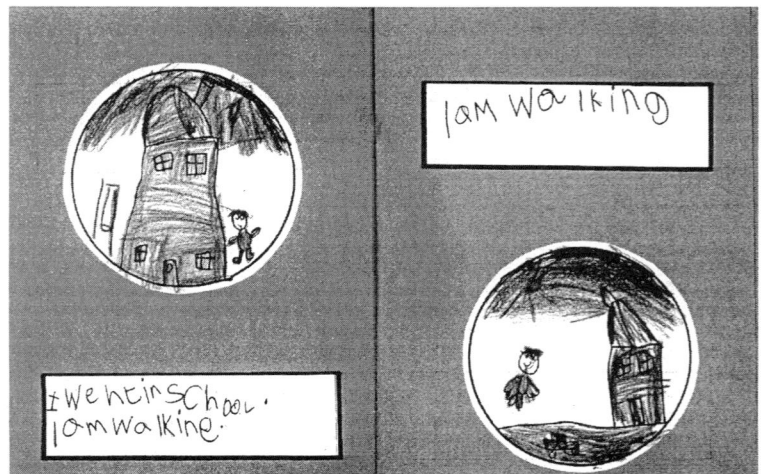

I am walking

I we htin school.
I am walking.

I woke up early, I got dressed and I went for a long walk. About half an hour later I came across a lovely little village. I noticed a beautiful church across the road. It had a tall steeple and colourful stained glass windows.

The Village Boy Family Album Natalie (aged 11)

Lost in Space group work (aged 14)

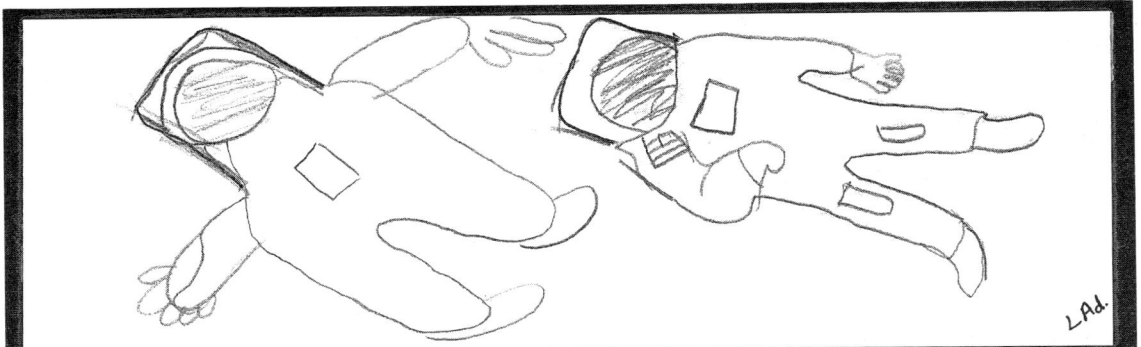

A robotic voice spoke to us.
"You are now 200,000 miles from Earth and heading for Mars."

Even so, Lee and John could not wait to try on a pair of space suits and open the hatch.

They were sucked out into space because they had forgotten to fasten their life-lines to the ship. We thought we had seen the last of John and Lee.

Computer designed books

Florida was produced on the word-processing and graphics program of a computer. Using the computer's mouse demands a set of drawing skills very different to those used in drawing with a pencil on paper. Holly was able to rearrange the block of text in the area provided until she found it visually satisfying.

Prescribed page formats

Giving children a precise page layout can suggest both the structure of a narrative and the way it is presented. Beth was given a four-page book format and fitted her drafted text and illustrations about a lost lamb into the prescribed spaces. When asked if it was difficult to do this, she replied, 'No, once I started writing it [the story] seemed to fit itself on the page ... I knew what I was going to put in the boxes [illustrations] before I did them.'

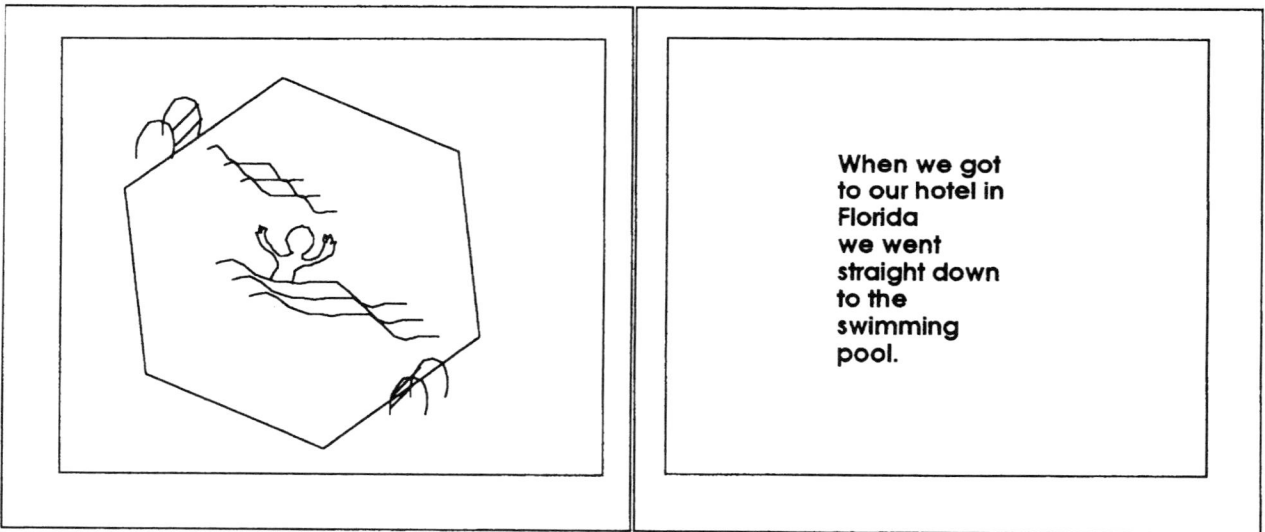

When we got to our hotel in Florida we went straight down to the swimming pool.

Florida Holly (aged 10)

Prescribed book format

The lost lamb

One day I was walking out on a pier when I heard a bleating from behind a rock. I went towards where the sound came from. I found it, lying there helpless. It was a lamb, small and thin. "Oh you poor thing"

I cried getting out my handkerchief. There was a small wound. I wrapped my handkerchief round it's wound. It gave

The Lost Lamb Beth
(aged 7)

another faint bleat. I understood. It's mother was somewhere near. I turned round and saw the mother. I sank down relieved that I had found her. I carried the lamb to her. She licked me. I went back home feeling pleased, proud and happy with

myself. In bed I had a dream about it. But, in my dream it had a scary bit in. But then I woke up and forgot about it.

Beth Jones.

The strip cartoon

Jan Ormerod (1992) found that by redefining the conventional narrative of her book *The Story of Chicken Licken* (1988) as a strip cartoon, the narrative was made more approachable to a young audience. Speech bubbles are commonly used by children in illustrations, but there has to be a certain logic to their use if confusion is to be avoided. The speech bubble also has to be accommodated by the picture area without disrupting the picture's composition.

Anansi the Spiderman is another prescribed layout, but designed as a strip cartoon by Jennifer's class teacher on a school computer. It has helped Jennifer to plan an illustrated narrative. Only in the middle section does she come unstuck with the technique of 'ballooning' the dialogue. Where in the box to place the dialogue is always a tricky question. Often, the sky area – notoriously difficult to make interesting in pictures – is conveniently selected for it.

As Beth's story above was nudged into a sequence of words and images by the prescriptive page layout, so variations of box shapes can stimulate and formulate the cartoon-oriented narrative. *John's Rocket* was written by one pupil and illustrated by two other pupils. Notice how the prescribed 'boxes' have influenced the plot. (The prescribed sheets from which *John's Rocket* was derived are published in *Book Pack 3 – Introducing illustration to children*, The Book Art Project, 1993.)

Tentative beginnings

These examples of children's work indicate the emergence of elementary design skills. Sarah and Lisa were given the most simple of directions – to work within a border – whereas Michael learnt through a growing awareness of his own design mistakes, and Zadir took to it from a storyboard approach. We have also seen that text and artwork can be prepared in isolation and then designed into a book form, and that teacher-prescribed page layouts can equip pupils with a unique guide to devising a narrative. Basic approaches to good page design can be taught, but like most things which appear quite simple, on the surface at least, the psychology of page design is more complex and enthralling the deeper one goes into it.

Anansi the Spiderman Jennifer (aged 8)

Joltn's Rocket

By Helen Kenny and Kate Nichol.

John climbed up into the rocket

Suddenly it rose into the air

John took command of the rocket

He looked out of the window and realised that he was in space.

John's Rocket

The rocket landed on a strange planet.

On it lived strange creatures who made lollipops.

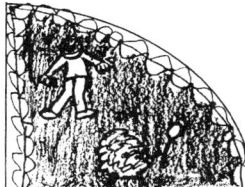

John ran down a tunnel into their lollipop factory. He heard the lollipop men chasing after him,

So he picked up the largest and most colourful lollipop he could find...

and ran to the edge of the planet.

He jumped off and using the lollipop as a parachute landed back on earth.

Chapter 3

A Closer Look at the Page

It is a strange fact that so many teachers neglect the obvious gain in readability, apart from other aesthetic considerations, when a page of writing has proper margins. One has an uncomfortable precipice sensation when reading 'school writing' that runs to the edge of the page.

Leonard Marsh (1970)

The unmarked areas of a printed page have their own rules. They have as much to say as the marks they surround or are surrounded by. To write clearly what they mean to communicate, children need to see and then organise the space in their pages.

Defining margins

Starting as early as possible, children should acquire the habit of drawing a border to the page before starting to write or draw. Measuring and drawing margins can be boring, but drawing around card templates cut to about 1cm smaller than the page size in an A6 book, and progressively wider margins for larger books, reduces the tedium (see Appendix 1). If there is one template per two pupils, the time spent on preparing the page for writing and drawing is considerably reduced. The empty space around a panel of work sets it off. The surrounding emptiness simultaneously holds the imagery securely *in* the page and yet pushes it *out*, accents it.

Page noise

Without margins, a feeling of chaos and 'page noise' is projected from the page. Hayley's spread is cacophonous – it yells at you! Of course, it isn't just the absence of margins that makes all this noise – see, too, the uncompromising thick black fibre-tipped pen lines and the general messiness of everything.

The Elephant's Christmas again suffers from the uncompromising brashness of the fibre-tipped pen work. The unbroken artwork looks more like a decorative headband than a sequence of contextual illustrations.

In Liam's case, it is the text which appears to be one continuous strip across the top half of the book.

My Christmas Book
Liam (aged 8)
▶

What is Down There?
  Hayley (aged 8)

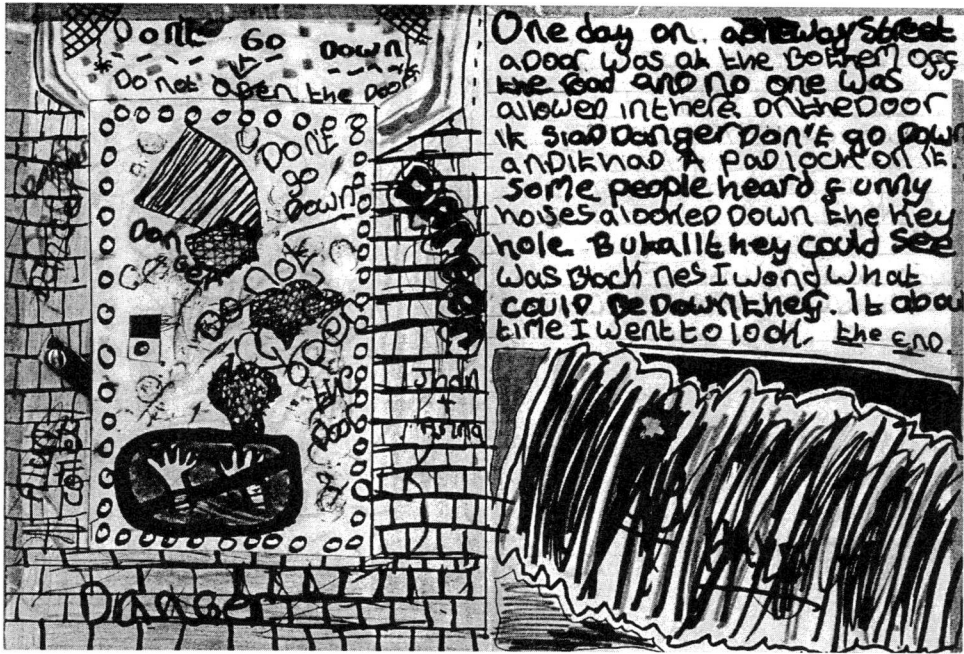

 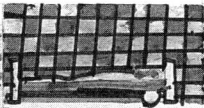   

The Elephant's Christmas Gemma and Katrina (aged 8)

Tidying the page

Lyndsey's book lacks margins so the text is difficult to read. The illustrations appear to be slipping off the page, because they rest on the bottom edge. This sense of falling is accentuated by the uneventful horizontal middle space on the first page which gives the impression that it is from here that the picture of Rama and Sita has slipped. Similarly, the wide vertical space in the centre of the next illustration makes it look as if the two characters portrayed have been forced apart to the extremities of the page. Lyndsey's teacher helped her to restructure *Rama and Sita*. The space has been redistributed; the text has been ordered into a block, the first illustration moved upwards and the figures of the second inwards. Scansion is an altogether more harmonious and satisfying experience for the reader.

Rama and Sita
Lyndsey (aged 9)

One day Rama went for a walk and he saw a girl and her name was sita and they went for a walk rama said will you marry me yes I will said sita they walked through the magic

forest when they got to the palace and sita said to her Father can I marry rama if he can thread the Bow Rama was taken to a Room sitas Father said if you can thread the Bow you can have sita so Rama was left to do it in an hour he did it sitas

Rama and Sita
restructured

One day Rama went for a walk and he saw a girl and her name was sita and they went for a walk. Rama said Will you marry me? Yes I will said sita. They walked through the magic

forest. When they got to the palace and sita said to her Father can I marry rama if he can thread the Bow? Rama was taken to a Room. Sitas Father said if you can thread the Bow you can have sita. so Rama was left to do it in an hour. He did it. Sitas

Margin balance

Margins must have a comfortable width or depth for them to work efficiently. Emma's margins, while better than none at all, are too narrow.

Text surrounded by a border requires a margin, otherwise the words collide with the border. Louise's list of Christmas events is too close to the border for visual comfort. However, the opposite is true of illustrations which are conventionally edged with line borders.

Left and right space

Problems occur when the 'ideal' left and right margin proportions discussed earlier are flouted. If the left side margin is smaller than the right, it gives the impression of either the left margin being too small for the page or the right side one being too large. Each one conditions how the other is perceived.

Top and bottom space

The text and illustrations in Tamara's book have been pushed down to accommodate numbering. This makes the upper margin wider than the lower one. As we have seen, a deeper bottom margin is traditional in book design; too deep an upper margin makes the picture look as if it has dropped from its rightful position on the page. The deeper bottom margin gives the impression of page balance. The gap between page number and frame should have been reduced, or – better still – the numbers placed at the foot of the page.

Numbering pages

The placing of page numbers is more important than might be thought. Inspecting at random twenty books from my bookshelves, I find that seven have numbers at the top, and thirteen have numbers at the bottom. There is also variation in the precise location of the numbers. Central placing is the classical position, but placing numbers on fore-edge corners is also quite popular. The last decade or two has seen bewildering experimentation in where, and in what form, page numbers can be incorporated into the page design. Try placing a number under or above a page grid and you will see that it immediately demands a space of its own. So, when designing a page, the placement of the page number should always be taken into account. Examine the examples of pupils' pages using numbers in this book and ask yourself: 'Is the page number of the right size and in the best position for the page design?'

Christmas
Louise (aged 9)

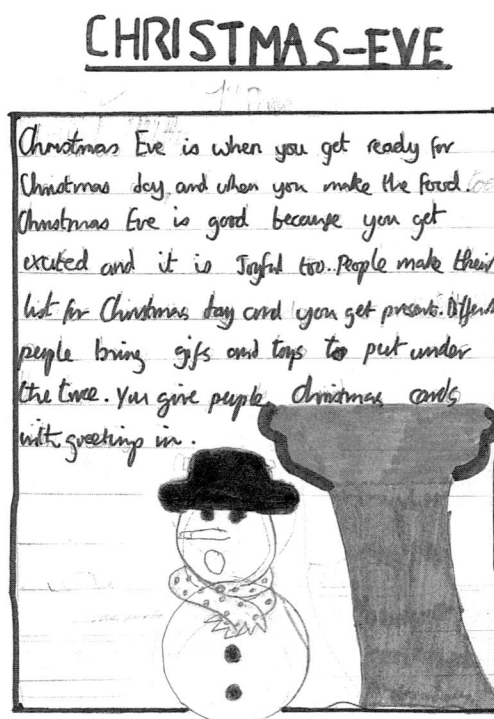

CHRISTMAS-EVE

Christmas Eve is when you get ready for Christmas day and when you make the food. Christmas Eve is good because you get excited and it is Joyful too. People make their list for Christmas day and you get presents. Different people bring gifts and toys to put under the tree. You give people christmas cards with greeting in.

Geneva
Emma (aged 8)

One day a little
girl called
Geneva asked
her mum if she
could have some
sweets to take to
her tree house.
Her mum said "Yes,
O.k." and gave her
a basket of sweets.
Her mum said "Make

How the Jungle Won Part 3
Tamara (aged 10)

4

saw a python hanging
from a tree infront of
them. Although they were
rough men they were
certainly cowards so
they clung onto one an-

5

other shivering, teeth chatt-
ering. At last they could
not stand up any more.
They dropped into the
undergrowth.
"Silence" roared
Dinko the lion, king of the
jungle. All of the courtiers
of the jungle had assem-
bled under the assem-
bling point which was
the weeping willow
tree which stood by
the pyrana stream. All

Nuances of page design

Subtleties of measuring are of immense importance. The following suggestions, which are general and so need not be taken as hard and fast rules, reinforce some of the points already made about visual balance.

Portrait orientation (depth greater than width)

- A half-page illustration looks well in the top half of a page (1). Placed in the bottom half it can look heavy – as if it is falling off the page (2). (However, for rhythmic balance illustrations are often placed here.)

- A page comprising solely a half-page block of text looks best with the text in the bottom half of the page. Placed in the top half it can appear as if there is something missing from beneath it.

- If the top margin is too generous the artwork/text appears to have slipped down and to be over-wide for the page (3).

- If the top margin is pushed further down towards the mid-point, the slipping effect disappears, but the block can still look hemmed in (4).

- On the single page, blocks moved to the right look unbalanced (5), but this is corrected by the double-page spread. The central fold compensates for the narrower gutter margins (6).

- Half-page portrait blocks on portrait pages create vertical gaps on either side (7). Consequently, landscape blocks fit more comfortably into portrait pages than portrait blocks (1–6).

Landscape orientation (width greater than depth)

Most of the observations about portrait page design apply to the landscape page also. But there are some notable differences:

- Half-page landscape blocks on landscape pages create unusually wide vistas (8).

- In books of unusually large dimensions the text should be arranged in two columns. Otherwise the lines are too long for comfortable reading (8–10).

- Portrait blocks are visually more acceptable, particularly if balanced by an adjacent column of text (9).

- Landscape illustration blocks can be effective occupying part of one or both columns (10).

Portrait or landscape?

Roxana's spread, in which square blocks are placed in the centre of landscape pages, looks awry: the insufficient horizontal margins make the unusually wide vertical margins look even wider, obliging the eye to travel an inordinate distance from illustration to text. To avoid this, the square blocks could have been presented on a square page or a portrait page, or they could have been moved closer to the centre fold, creating 'luxury' margins.

Unless children trim down standard sheets of paper (which are always supplied in rectangles) it is impossible for them to make basic books comprising anything other than rectangular pages. In the portrait-orientated book it makes an attractive, off-square spread, but the cinemascopic expanse of landscape pages needs special treatment if it is not to appear unreasonably wide. Michael Foreman exploits this wonderfully in *War Boy* (1991) by using sweeping rural and urban landscape illustrations.

Both landscape and portrait formats have strengths and weaknesses, and the sensitive designer can make written and graphic material fit either satisfactorily. Examine the portrait/landscape design of books in your school library and with your class identify the techniques employed. Can you find a book for which, in your view, the choice of orientation is wrong? Does the class agree?

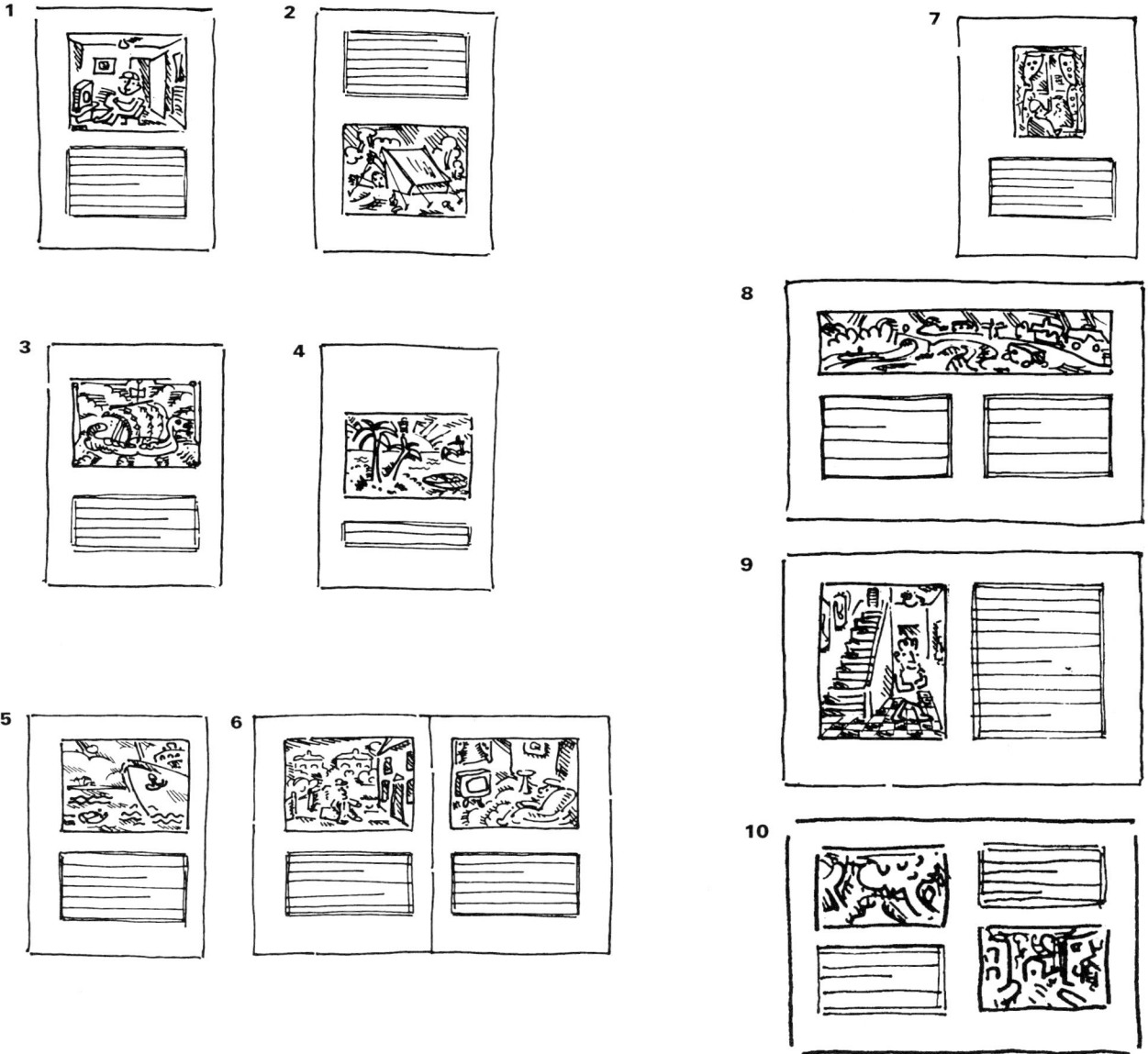

The Tree House
Roxana (aged 10)

"Too curious my girl. Honestly I only come here once a year and still I get interrupted. I don't know why I come here!"
"How come you're here?" I asked.
"This is my home, well, was my home until some horrible creatures, a bit like you, ransacked it!" he replied not looking a bit pleased about it.
"Yes it is a bit of a mess," I said looking around the tree house. I looked at my watch. Was it that time already or was my watch fast?
"I better be going," I said.
I told him that I might come back and see him the next day but I'd gone and was running away before he had a chance to tell me he wasn't going to be there tomorrow because he was going back to space. As soon as I got home everyone awoke and I forgot about the strange creature alltogether.

Square books

Square-shaped books are more common in children's publishing than in publishing generally. Although the symmetry of the square suggests that it is a design asset, blocks of text and artwork tend in reality to be better accommodated organically by rectangles than squares. Referring once more to Mick Inkpen's *Billy's Beetle*, by using two square pages as, effectively, one rectangular landscape spread, and by freely crossing the gutter with artwork, the author produces a very satisfactory effect. Similarly, the illustrations in *Luxury Holidays* appear exceptionally narrow by being continued over the whole spread, but the tactic can, as in this case, be very effective.

Juggling shapes

On the whole, Kirsteen has made a good job of fitting her material into the square page. 'Spooky menu', 'blood shake', 'mice cream', 'worm pie' and 'bat on a bap' look at ease in the square.

Unusual book shapes

In the eternal attempt to escape from convention, triangular-shaped books are on the ascendant in children's publishing. (For an example of this see *The Tombs of the Pharaohs* by Sue Clarke, 1994.) Certain kinds of pop-up books fold down snugly into the triangular shape. Sarah has taken advantage of the triangular shape to suggest the characters portrayed within it. The bed is drawn almost at the angle of the hypotenuse. Words are carefully spaced into progressively widening lines.

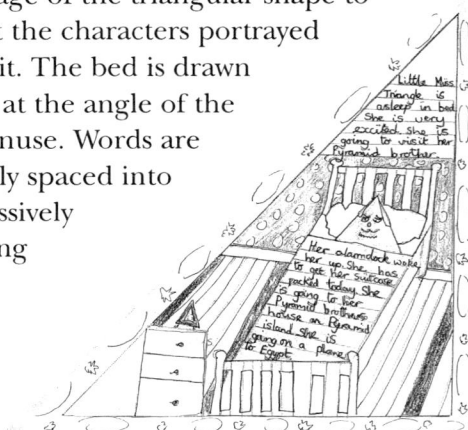

Panel shape variations

A page template with rounded top corners can make a world of difference to pupil motivation, particularly for children like Christopher with learning difficulties. 'In appraising the written work in their self-made books,' said Natasha, his teacher, 'what was most apparent was the style and presentation of handwriting within the templated area, compared to the back cover where the template was absent. The rear cover represented a standard sheet of plain paper, but the templated page with the curved border encasing the children's writing highlighted the space and made it more important to them.'

Grouping words

How children arrange words inside borders or frames is highly significant for their ultimate legibility. Research indicates that excessively long lines of words cause a sharp increase in the number of regressions (reading a line twice), while short lines make it hard to maintain the continuity of what is being read (J. Biggs,1977).

In the computer age, typography, once the preserve of the publishing fraternity, is everybody's business. In published children's books the readability of words is of paramount importance. Some typefaces give more pronounced word shapes than others. Likewise, the spaces between words influence the ease with which children scan them. Some children's books have excessive space between words. Rather than making reading easier, which is presumably the typographer's intention, these spaces destroy the continuity which is essential in linking one word to the next.

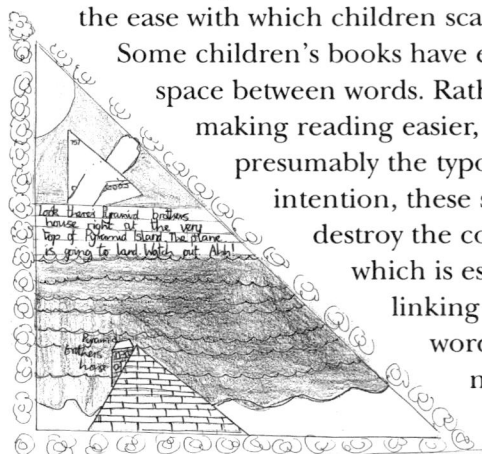

Little Miss Triangle visits Pyramid Brother Sarah (aged 10)

All of a sudden the "Luxury holidays" boat struck a massive rock on the sea bed and started to sink. It sank very fast. People dived off and swam to the island. But the people on the island didn't even help.

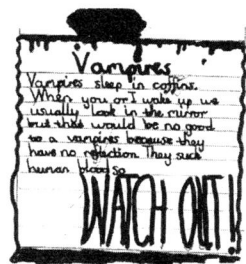

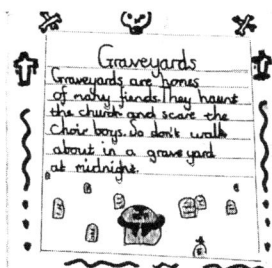

Spooks Kirsteen (aged 10)

The Body Snatcher (page spread and back cover) Christopher (aged 9)

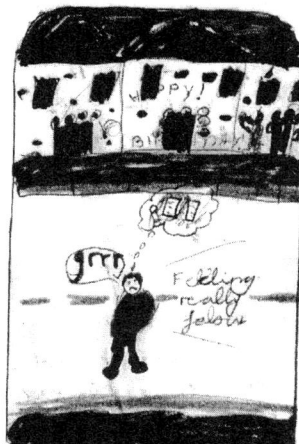

Children are sometimes encouraged to put generous spaces between words when learning to write (a 'finger space'), but, as Sue Walker (1992) points out, word spaces that are too wide are likely to interrupt pupils' reading of their own writing.

Another aspect of spacing is whether the setting is to be justified or unjustified. In the former, both sides of the block of text are straight, and word spacings vary from line to line. This creates a tidy and regular shape for the block, but tends to interrupt the reading flow. Unjustified settings, in which word spaces remain constant and the right-side edge is ragged, are easier to follow. Although it is difficult to lay down rules about the spaces between lines, the larger the typeface the longer the line length needs to be and the greater the distance between lines. Vertical space – that between headings, sub-headings and text – is as important as horizontal space and inadequate or incorrectly proportioned space between sections of type can determine whether or not the decoding process is an easy or difficult task for the reader.

Looking at some of the common problems associated with children writing into their book pages, Sue Walker's observations about the typography in the books they read are relevant, particularly at a time when the trend is for pupils to write for specific audiences. Whether writing for their peers or for younger children, they need to be aware of the way words are presented. Teaching pupils to write justified scripts in some circumstances and unjustified in others, or to plan the vertical spacing of texts that conform to a mathematical formula, may be more relevant to the young adult than to the child. Nevertheless, Walker is right when she asserts that younger pupils should be aware of such things in the books they read.

Organising lines of writing

Using paper with printed lines seems an obvious way of making straight lines of writing, but it is rare, in a book setting at least, for it to look pleasing. Uncompromising printed lines somehow look too regimented, too restrictive. Some young children have a natural propensity for writing in straight lines. Joanne's text – with accurately judged horizontal lines, placement within the border, gaps between words and well sized page borders – is easy and indeed pleasurable to read. Drawing parallel lines for words to rest on, following the practice of the medieval scribes, can be boring and time consuming.

Line control

Writing in straight lines without the use of ruled lines comes with practice and is most successful with short lines of writing. Even then, words tend to slope after a while but, providing the gradient is not too steep, the homespun appearance can have its own appeal.

When lines are drawn they should be made lightly with a pencil and, if preferred, rubbed out after use. Care should be taken to avoid leaving too much or too little space between the lines for the writing. Only rarely can drawn lines work as an acceptable part of the design. Vicky's text looks insignificant against the lines in thick black ink. But Paul's strongly individualistic handwriting has the vigour to hold its own against the sharply inscribed lines it rests on.

The Brownie
Joanne (aged 6)

Once upon a time There was a brownie called Joanne. Joanne had a baby brownie. and if you lift the loch you will see Joanne. Monday it was sung Tuesday it was ringing Wendsday it was brownies Joanne went to brownies. and her baby went with her. but the baby Did not like brownie one bit. the baby went out side and tried to get home. but she went into a wood and got lost She saw a fox and the fox woß a good fox

The Boy who Liked Snow
Vicky (aged 9)

One day there was a boy called Paul and he liked Snow. One day he went out to play in the Snow and there was some ice and he slipped. Into a hole.

Then he Climbed out of the hole

The Rune Sword part 2 Paul (aged 10)

THE RUDE SWORD

Three people were picked to find this sword. Adrianon a hu-man brave, clever, and skilled, Randolph a Dwarf, skilled mechanic and fighter Lauier a magician very clever but weak in battle.

Chapter 1

As they finally set foot on Varken island where the sword was supposedly hidd-en, if it was there, was a peril-ous journey ahead. and indi-eed it was far within it

VARKEN

BEACH RIVER.

"Clang"

-ve minutes after they had landed they were under attack a horde of skelet-ons appeared. Adrianon was cut badly on the shou-lders but still managed to beat his opponent while Lauier simply clicked his fingers and the sand swall-owed his foe up, but he still had skeleton Hawion to deal with, he quickly turn-ed, fired two fireballs and he was victorious. Meanwhile

Drawn lines which vary in width and are not parallel also weaken the success of a block of writing, as in Gemma's book. Unless the line widths are reasonably accurate it is best to have none at all. Running out of space at the bottom of the page, with lines forced closer together, is, as we have already seen, another common problem encountered by young book artists. These hazards show the need for children to have a system of page planning which starts at the drafting stage.

Conservative words: liberal illustrations

Another common difficulty in children's book art is visualising how a section of script will appear when juxtaposed with an illustration. Professional designers tend to plan illustrations around text rather than text around illustrations; there is much more flexibility in arranging visual material than groups of words. Words are visually intransigent: they can be hard to read if not designed into a logical shape. The content of an illustration, by contrast, can be arranged in a hundred different ways, pushed into unusual shapes, squeezed, stretched, flattened, spread out all over the page, or miniaturised into a cameo. In the hands of a sensitive artist the arrangement will look well designed, indeed inevitable – one could not imagine it any other way.

Separate identities

The last lines of Michaela's script collide with the illustrations because she failed to plan her space allocations. Apart from being visually dissatisfying, it is difficult to read the bottom line and descenders like 'g' and 'y' are forced into the picture area. Leaving adequate space between writing and pictures is vital for the page to 'work'. Something else worth referring to here is that each letter in Michaela's text is coloured. Should pupils be given the freedom to ' play' with the sheer beauty of letter forms in this way, or should readability be the only criterion?

Progressing in stages

John's first spread has been written without guide lines and as such is not badly presented, but compare it to his second attempt at the same piece of work, where a border has been drawn and lines prepared for writing. 'Page consciousness' has made him more aware of the letter forms as he writes them and how they fit the designated space. What is also significant is that this refining process has made him think about the text itself; he was not able to include all his copy, so he has been forced to reduce the number of words. This refining and selecting process has improved the style of his writing, both in content and penmanship.

Handwriting

In the nineteenth century, when good handwriting, like cleanliness, was next to godliness, children were taught to reproduce copperplate handwriting in their copy books. This book shows an array of handwriting styles, some better formed than others, and some fitting the book form better than others. Words have to be drawn and placed accurately for them to realise fully the meaning they hold. Distances always have to be judged – is there enough space to fit the words in? – a challenge for all writers and signmakers, whatever their age.

Michaela's book (discussed above) demonstrates problems with word spacing. Many of the spaces are too great, reducing the number of words to the line. The line 'rhythm' is further disrupted by none of the words starting at the beginning of the specified margin line. Resulting large gaps at the end of most lines make for uncomfortable reading.

Rama and Sita
Gemma (aged 9)

My Adventure in Space
First version
John (aged 9)

My Adventure in Space
Second version

*The Boy who Invented
an Egg Box Robot*
Michaela (aged 8)

Mind-eye intelligence

The right edge of Gemma's column in her book is almost justified. She is acquiring the skill of adjusting the size of the gaps between words as she writes. Although there may be too many lines to the page, the harmony of letter forms and accurate spacing between words here integrate the page into a visual unity.

Breaking words

A common problem with handwriting is the uncompromising barrier of the centrefold. Mature writers take this 'wall' into account, judging the available space ahead intuitively. 'Breaking' words is of course inevitable. When the division is between syllables hyphens are generally acceptable, but not when breaks are placed elsewhere in a word. In Timothy's page of writing the breaks come in all the wrong places, thus making reading difficult.

Stylish writing

The revival of italic handwriting in the twentieth century was influenced by Edward Johnston's *Writing, Illuminating and Lettering*

(1906). It is a tradition kept alive today in our classrooms by those teachers who contend that, if something is worth writing, it is worth writing with calligraphic style. Another pioneer in the field, Alfred Fairbank (1949), argued that in handwriting there is always a tug-of-war between economy, as a time-saver, and legibility. In an overcrowded curriculum this is an important point: can time be 'spared' for the acquisition of a model handwriting style? For some children perhaps, but for most the aim must be the acquisition of a legible and easily rendered personal writing style.

Computers can provide children with medieval-type fonts and joined-up italic handwriting. However, electronic techniques, time-saving and essential to communication as they are, do not have the aesthetic appeal of a delightful piece of handwriting, which can say so much about the person who has made it. 'People present themselves to the world through their handwriting and are inevitably judged by it,' says Rosemary Sassoon (1990), a leading expert in children's handwriting.

John said come on get in a line behind me, and they all went in a line behind John and went in. They went in to a room and it had spiders, cobwebs and some old curtains with holes in them. Then they went in another room and that was the same. In fact all of the rooms were like that, all except one that was up stairs, that they went in last. In that room there were a bed, a chair, a dressing table with things on it and a wardrobe full of clothes

Nelly Meets a Ghost
Gemma (aged 8)

In the fantastic car there is an engine that runs by itself.
When you go to the seaside the car changes into a hovercraft. The car can change into any car in the world. What you want, it wil-

Breaking words
Timothy (aged 8)

Pages of italic script
Ross (aged 9)

to school "AND WHAT TIME DO YOU CALL THIS?" well...well... I sliped in the sand sir, honestly "NEVER MIND THE EXCUSES, IN MY OFFICE NOW" right you can start on the floors, "yes sir" "I had to miss out on breakfast that morning. Suddenley the door opened "right boy I'll let you off as this is the first time you've been late but don't go thinking your Father won't hears about this "Phew lucky escape. It must be at least noon by now' so I went to see Dad down at the canal "Hello son do us a favour will yer "sure what do you wont?" fetch us some firewood after that we could go fishing "cool I said.

CHAPTER 2
Going fishing

HERE you go Dad thanks son all set we should be back for two cocobeans off we went "here's your rod, so what have you done at school today" oh you know the usual "no I don't know what you mean by usual "well sword fights" I see, Right lets get fishing your mum should have dinner ready by the time we get back." Hey dad I got something "pull it" what kind is it Dad youve got a gooden there Quaaxochitl. It was around three cocobeans when we got back" later than we thought, hey son WELL" SORRYEE "don't be cheaky just what is the matter with you today" well I skidded on the gravel an I had to

Harmonious lines

What is particularly fascinating about the handwritten illustrated book is the relationship between the word forms, as art, and the penmanship of the drawings. In Eleanor's book, both 'languages' combine into one visually aesthetic unity.

There were two terrible twins called Prunella and Patricia who were always fighting. Whenever one had something the other one wanted it.

2

Patricia got a nice blue dress for her birthday. When Prunella saw it she wanted it. She tried it on but it was too small.

3

Her mum said to her 'you will be late for school' But Prunella couldn't get the dress off. When she went in the classroom all the pupils laughed at

4

her. She got sent to the head for not wearing uniform. As a punishment, she had to run around the playground fifty times.

5

The Terrible Twins ▲
Eleanor (aged 10) ▼

Prunella soon got tired running, and collapsed on the grass, tangled up in her dress. She had only been round the playground ten

6

times. Prunella had learnt her lesson. She never took other people's property without asking again.

7

Eleanor is ten years old, likes drawing and is a pupil at Beaver Rd Junior School, Manchester

© Eleanor Diggle 1994
The Book Art Project
The Manchester Metropolitan
University M20 2RR

The *The Book Art Project*
Children's
Press
MANCHESTER
METROPOLITAN
UNIVERSITY

8

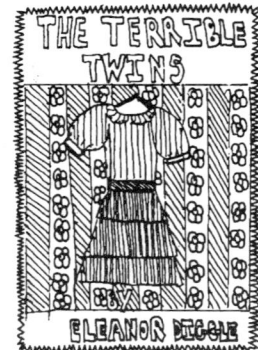

58

Pupils working on their books

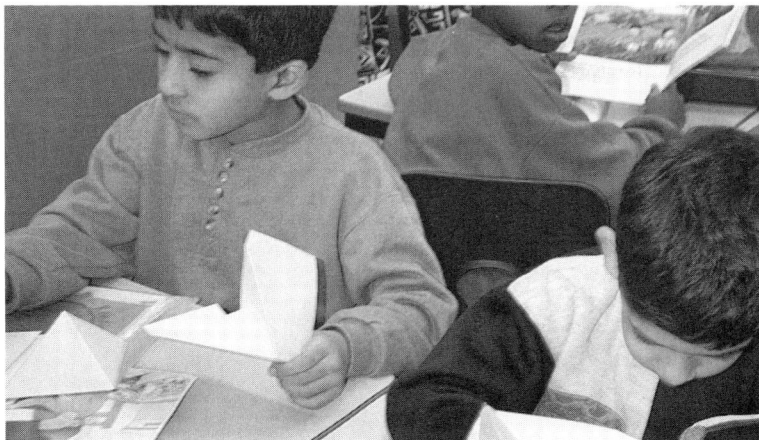

Pacing the spacing

Some children will find preparing texts and artwork for book production arduous and will consequently lose interest. The teacher has to assess when it is best to advise a pupil to redesign material and when improvements should be processed gradually in successive projects. The computer has an advantage over the hand-drawn page in that areas of type and graphics can be moved effortlessly about the screen. But making books can stimulate in children the determination to get it exactly right, so that the redrawing process is not a burden, but a step towards a self-selected goal. As a Manchester teacher put it, 'Children of all learning abilities sense their own strengths and weaknesses, but the book arts lift them up to a level of expectation that they see as being within their reach.'

Decorative borders

Margins can be seen as designed space, and borders as decorative or quasi-decorative 'frames' around illustrations or text. Arnheim (1974) sees ornament primarily as a visual form that is subordinated to a larger whole which it enriches. He points out that it is illogical for ornament to be a work of art in its own right, any more than a work of art can act as ornament. However, the regular pattern of ornament serves art in a uniquely enriching and satisfying way. Arnheim implies that this repetitive enrichment is essential to our psychological well-being and erudition.

As a form of applied art, ornament appears in book design from the earliest codices or manuscript volumes to the books of the present day. In the nineteenth century, page decorations – 'printer's ornaments' as they came to be known – often over-embellished and suffocated pages. In the experimental ambience of present-day children's book illustration, not a few exponents – Peter Bowman (1986), for example – have challenged the conventionally passive role of the border and, by elevating it to the status of illustration, have given it a life of its own.

Types of border

Line frame

Double frames to illustrations and a single frame to the block of text make a very satisfying enhancement to Sarah's spread. The bold colour and shapes of the original artwork needed the extra support provided by the coloured-in double border. This would have been unnecessary for the block of text.

The border of *Pirates* is so thick that the copy looks suffocated by it. Instead of enhancing the content of the pages, this border diminishes it.

Lyndsey's border is thin enough not to be too obtrusive, the overall appearance gaining from the background space around the text.

Mummy Sarah (aged 9)

Pirates Richard (aged 7)

Trick on Bear Lyndsey (aged 8)

Embellished borders

Borders which are free in style, with well-spaced basic motifs, are appropriate for topical subjects like Kirsteen's self-portrait. She has successfully incorporated lettering, text, artwork and border into an integrated image.

Going Back Kirsteen (aged 8) ▶

▼

I was born

On Sunday the 8th of November 1981 I was born in Panteg hospital. I started to walk about a year later. When I was two (1983) my brother Iain was born.

1981–1983

THE SLIDE

When I was around the age of four we went to a local park. My mum was talking to a friend and I went down a slide on my front and fell off the slide head first. I had to have stitches.

1985

FRANCE

One year I went to France on holiday. Round the back of the caravan there was a small farm. I was looking at the goat and I bent down to pick some grass for it to eat and the goat started eating my hair!

1987

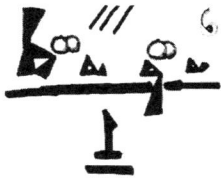

I started going gym when I was four. I am now ten and I have moved to a different gym. I go on a Saturday and on a Monday night. We do bar, beam and floor work. My most recent badge was my B.a.g.a one. B.a.g.a stands for British Amateur Gymnastics Association.

1991

Pickles

My mum and dad had told me that I was allowed to buy a pet. I wanted a baby rabbit. We went to look at some in Poynton. Then we went to a pet shop in Hazel Grove. They were selling kittens that were just a few weeks old. I had a look at them and I bought a black one with white paws. I called it Pickles.

1991

Pattern borders

The borders of Alison's book are overpowering, owing not so much to their thickness as to the uncompromisingly assertive and clumsily drawn motifs. The eye is so bombarded by the sharp and jagged design work, which bears no relationship to the theme, that the text pales into relative insignificance. With hindsight, and after consultation with her teacher, she softens the border on the third page and the appearance is more sensitive and complementary to the text.

The zig-zag borders to Elizabeth's book provide a simple, recurrent and rhythmic enrichment to the page.

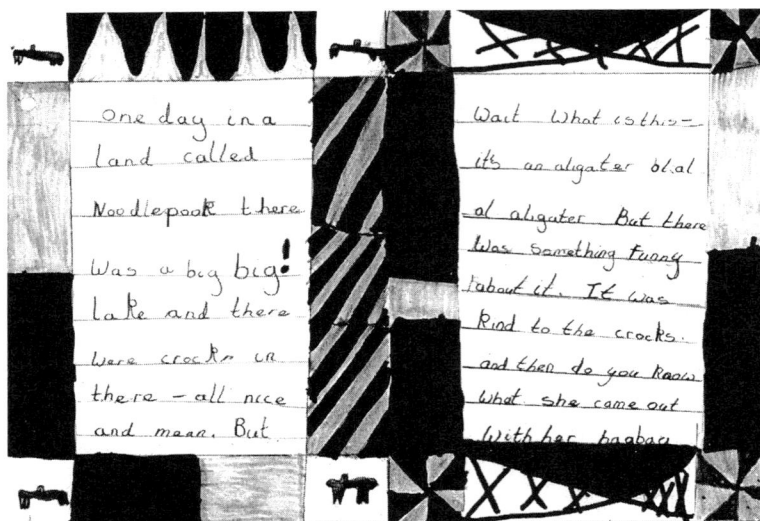

The Mysterious Noise
Elizabeth (aged 10)

Alli the Alligator Alison (aged 9)

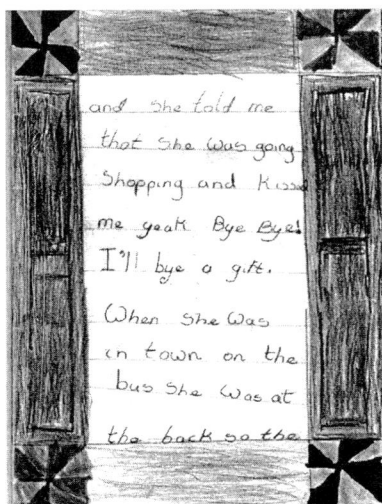

Thematic borders

The teddy bear motif provides the border material for the second page and hanging stars for the following page of Nat's book. Both devices relate to the story of the toy shop and are freely improvised around the page area without a pre-drawn framework.

Asymmetrical borders

A vertical strip of page ornament has 'spiced up' the otherwise conventional appearance of Tamara's text. The central 'gutter' of the page spread is usually a no-go area in book design, but Louise has spontaneously used this area in her book as a decorative sub-title.

Mr Eds Toy Shop
Nat (aged 5)

18

give you a chance to plead. You may begin". So Bongle began his story begining at the mud bath and ending at the time he heard the two monsters (as he called the two men). The lion king listened to the Hippo's story with interest and at the end of it he said: "That is a terrible dis-

19

aster, Bongle, we must do something about it and I have a good idea. The animals will all be covered in mud and will charge onto

How the Jungle Won Part 3
Tamara (aged 10)

Art
Louise (aged 9)

Background texture

Background pictorial artwork or texture can be attractive, providing it does not compete with what rests on it. Insensitively presented, it looks confusing: one cannot see the picture for the writing, or the writing for the picture.

Sarah's pencil crayon work provides a soft 'bed' of figurative imagery for the words and pictures to lie on. All six pages of her origami book are reproduced because it is a good example of continuity of design. Several different strategies for presenting information are used; the text and visuals harmonise thoughtfully with one another and, at the same time, keep the mind of the reader alert.

Preoccupied by precision

Very small faults can often wreck children's design work. We have seen that the matter of a few millimetres can change the appearance and readability of a block of handwriting enormously. Badly drawn or ill-placed page numbers, above or below, can shatter beautifully drawn artwork. Inappropriate border designs distract the eye from the information they are meant to enhance. With help, children see these things for themselves, think more clearly about what they are trying to do and experience the pleasure of presenting ideas to a reading public in the best possible way.

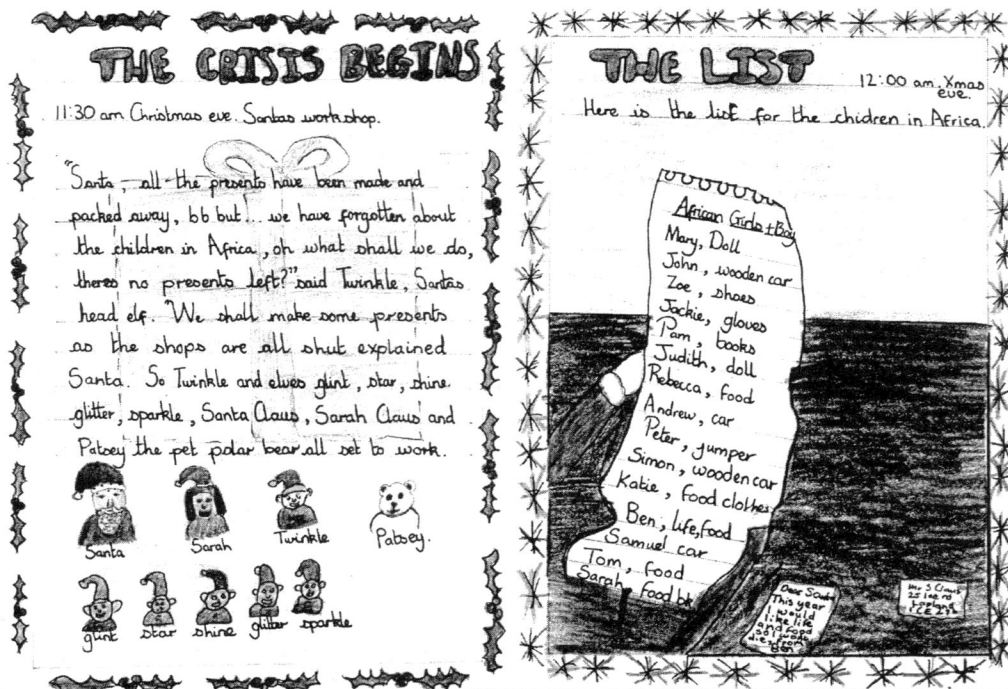

Santa's Problem Sarah (aged 10)

GETTING STARTED

Christmas eve 1:00 pm.

Santa made some wooden cars for the boys, Sarah knitted some wooley Santa jumpers, Twinkle made some little shoes, Glint made the dolls for the girls. Shine drew some pictures and made picture books. From candle wax Star made some wax crayons. Glitter (a good cook) made some cakes for the familys who need food. Sparkle made the wrapping paper and started wrapping up! Patsey the Polar bear loaded the sleigh, before they knew everything was ready.

SETTING OFF

"Give the children my love", said Sarah Claus, kissing Santa. "Bye everyone" said Santa as he flew into the air.

POOR BEN

After a while Santa landed in Africa he was just going down the chimney when he heard a faint sobbing. It was Ben Lombard. "Whats the matter Ben", asked Santa. "Its just I havent no food, no water, no decent clothes and very soon I will die of starvation" Ben said sadly.

OFF HOME

Merry Christmas Merry Christmas

Santa was feeling very sorry for Ben. "Where are you parents Ben?" asked Santa. They dived a mmonth ago, answered Ben. Santa gave Ben his presents a picture book, crayons car, cakes, jumpers, shoes and a little book on Christmas trees of which Santa had found. "How would you like to come and live with Sarah, the elves and I in Lapland Ben?" asked Santa. "Oh I would, thanks, answered Ben. So Ben and Santa delivered all the presents to the other African children. Then they went back to Lapland and Santa, Sarah, the elves and Ben lived happily ever after.

Merry Christmas Merry Christmas Merry Christmas Merry Christmas Merry Christmas Merry Christmas

Chapter 4

Designing Book Covers

The purpose of the [book] jacket today is not so much to protect as to sell. It is a special kind of poster.

Ruari McLean (1980)

The cover of a book is both an advertisement for and a clue to its contents. Publishers are aware that however good a book is, if the cover fails to attract the book shop browser, it will remain unopened. This places an enormous responsibility on the cover designer, a point I try to get over to children when they design their own book covers. Of course, the cover may deliberately falsify the material inside. Alluring artwork on the cover of a paperback novel beguiles the prospective purchaser without necessarily contributing to or reflecting what the book has to say. The title must be crisp and engaging, for the customer may scan a book display for only a few seconds. Design enhances the title through engaging letter forms, and the artwork catches the eye through imagery and colour. One so easily tires of both convention and extravagance, yet book cover designers are simultaneously required to satisfy the conservative expectations of the general public, yet seduce them with the prospect of something new and challenging.

Shock treatment

Excluding words altogether from the cover of Maurice Sendak's *We are all down in the*

dumps with Jack and Guy (1993), locating the title on the back cover of *Puss in Boots* (1991, illustrated by Fred Marcellino), and omitting the author's name from the cover of Chris Van Allsburg's *The Polar Express* (1985) may all be intriguing ploys to shock the potential reader into a positive response. Is it that the art styles of Sendak and Allsburg are so widely recognised that the presence of the artist's name has become superfluous?

Unusually long or short titles provide another shock strategy, as with *We are all down in the dumps with Jack and Guy*. If long titles became the norm, their novelty value would wear off and we would tire of them. Conversely, Roald Dahl's title, *The BFG* (1982), strikes us because of its brevity, inviting the reader to question what the initials stand for.

Choosing the title

Children find original book titles hard to come by. Younger writers often give descriptive titles to their stories, for example, *A Day at the Seaside*, but older ones, influenced by what they read, can be more adventurous and use titles which appeal to the imagination or the senses, or arouse curiosity. Working with student teachers I find they, too, have difficulty in choosing good, crisp titles for their stories. Somehow *A visit to the Zoo* doesn't have the same pull as *Beware, Crocodiles!* Even better is the ambiguous *Crocodiles, Beware!* – who is at risk, the reader or the crocodiles? A student who produced a story originally entitled *Horace the Dentist* reduced it to just one word – *Ouch!* Such things are not as trivial as they may seem. Professional writers and copy editors spend much time and energy on such things. To them, composing a good title may seem almost as important as the writing of the story it heralds.

Conceiving covers

Children usually begin a story by writing the title – or they feel 'blocked' until they can think of one. They do not easily understand that a book's cover and title are just about the last things to concern a publisher at this stage. That is why I have placed this chapter towards the end of the book. That the cover should epitomise the whole book, and can therefore only be contemplated after the book has been written, is an intellectual abstraction. A nice way to look at it is for children to perceive designing the cover as a kind of prize for completing a book, for without that accomplishment the title has no meaning.

Designing covers

Being surrounded by books facilitates the search for a well designed cover. Children making books according to the traditions of bookbinding use a variety of decoration techniques on their covers – water colour and wax resist, marbling, potato prints, lino prints. Not surprisingly, these techniques are being rediscovered by commercial publishers who use styles from the past in a bid to reflect the nostalgic mood of the present.

While examining picture books with children it is worth asking questions like: *why*

did Shirley Hughes choose *that* particular title for her book? Why does such-and-such an incident from the story figure as the cover picture? With experience, children, like many a professional writer/illustrator, will find themselves contemplating and listing possible titles. Many ideas will be considered and rejected before sensing, '*This is it!*' With experience, they scan the plot for 'that unusual or extra-special incident' and enlarge it into what will become the cover feature.

Spotlight on the title

Pupils soon discover that it can take as long to design the lettering for a one-word cover title as it takes to write two pages of narrative. Whereas a slightly mis-spaced word in a sentence is barely noticed, the slightly off centre single word of the title *Sam* appears glaringly inept.

Sam
Daniel (aged 8)

Young book artists like Jessica so often relegate their names to the lower extremities of the cover. Is it children's unselfconsciousness that makes them pay so little attention to their names, as authors, on book covers? Having spent an hour or more on the title lettering, they merely scribe their names unobtrusively at the bottom like a signature.

Not yet conscious of the politics of publishing, where it is the writer, not the book, that is frequently being sold, these young authors are unaware of their social status. This lack of self-promotion also probably accounts for the fact that children rarely place their names at the top of a cover design. Searching through my large collection of children's self-made books, I came across only a handful in which pupils had done this, and then mainly from the early years of schooling. Could it be that the infant places his or her name at the top of the cover as a symbol of ownership, rather than as a statement about who wrote the book?

Strategies of cover design

Classifying A as title, B as illustration, C as author's (and illustrator's) name(s), the commonest cover format is A (top), B (middle) and C (bottom). The artwork centrepiece of the cover tends to dominate the design. The title comes next, but taking up less room, and the author's name last, taking less room still. (These last two categories can be reversed if the publisher regards the author as so celebrated that the title is 'inferior' to the writer's name.) Whatever is deemed the most important takes the top line, but doesn't have to be large in size.

Brian Wildsmith, one of Britain's most acclaimed children's book writer/ illustrators, has his name at the head of *Goat's Trail* (1986) but, because its position has precedence over the title further down,

it can afford to be smaller in size than the title. In this way both author and title balance themselves out in status terms.

Commonly, published children's books are an author/illustrator collaboration. But whose name should come first on the cover? Usually it is the writer's, but what happens if the illustrator is better known than the author, or there is disagreement as to who is the most famous? Publishers must heave a sigh of relief when the writer and illustrator are the same person.

Covers of published books

Teachers should refer to their school library for examples of the cover formats discussed below. They should not be difficult to find. See if there are any covers which take another path from conventional layouts. How successful have they been?

Words on covers are usually typeset, but some illustrators like to design the lettering themselves and incorporate it into the cover picture. Simon James (1991), in a book comprising fictitious letters between a little girl, Emily, and the ecological organisation, Greenpeace, writes the cover title – *Dear Greenpeace* – in a chunky fibre-tipped pen. This could have looked trite, and usually does when children do something like it, but in fact it blends perfectly with the cover artwork.

The Runaway Toys Jessica (aged 6)

Design forms

Title, artwork, author

Amanda's cover is a carefully proportioned design although the author's name is less well placed than the title.

Title, author, artwork

A study in contrast: the curvaceous panel holding the title and author contrasts with the background texture of snow on Claire's cover. The warmth of the yellow title panel is accented against the cold blue illustration area.

Artwork, title, author

Sarah's design came about by asking the class to draw boldly on their book covers a character or situation from their completed stories. Before commencing the artwork, the teacher asked the class to leave a space for the title and author's name at the bottom of the cover. Sarah discovered that she had only left enough room for her first name.

Author, title, artwork

Liz designed the three parts of the cover – title, author's name and artwork – separately on a sheet of paper, cut the lettering into strips, and then arranged them in various combinations before deciding on the CAB format. Her carefully planned name on two lines heads the cover, and leads the eye down through the title (in another form of lettering) to the simple but effective linear artwork.

Author, artwork, title

Jessica's boldly drawn name and title comfortably sandwich the butterfly illustration.

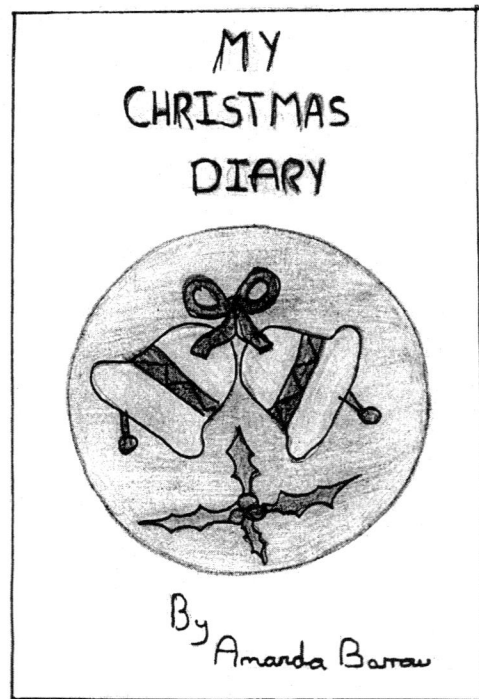

My Christmas Diary Amanda (aged 9)

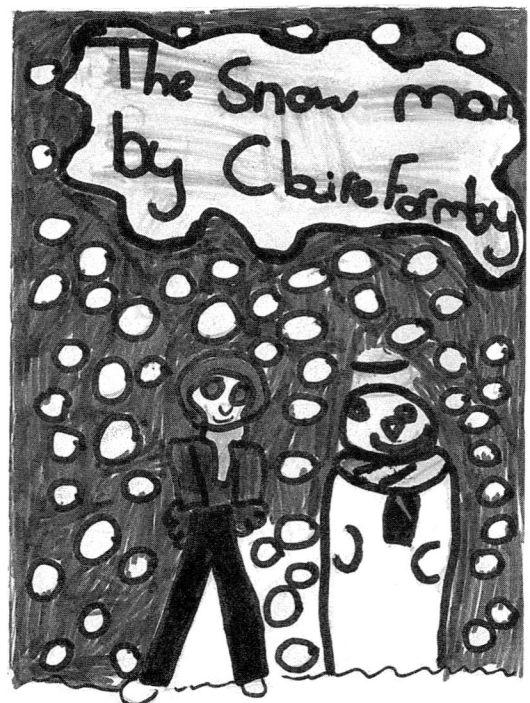

The Snow Man Claire (aged 8)

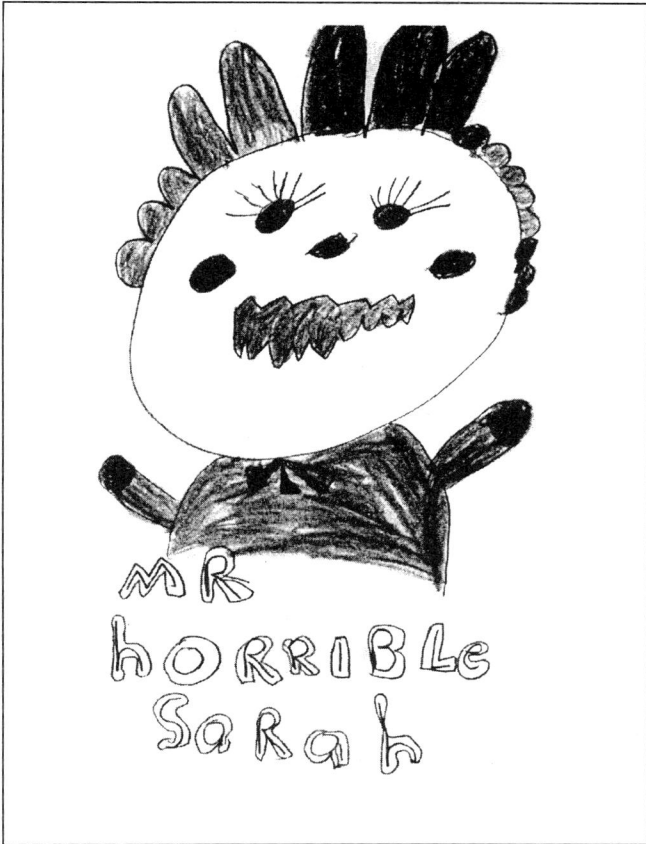

Mr Horrible Sarah (aged 6)

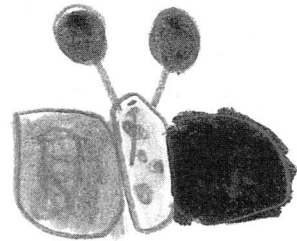

Spring Jessica (aged 5)

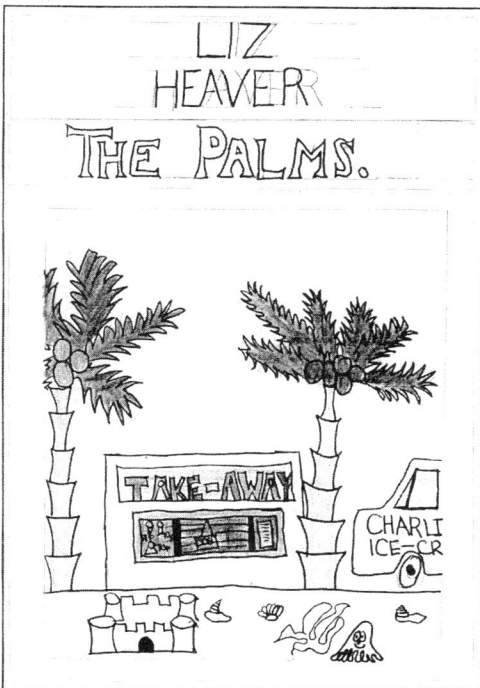

The Palms Liz (aged 10)

Vertical divisions

Alex has placed his title and name each side of the central image – a popular design alternative to the horizontal layering discussed so far. Lining titles up against the left side of the cover, as in this case, avoids the centring of letters.

Words over artwork

In addition to the title, author and artwork occupying discrete areas of the cover, the lettering can be placed on or in the total artwork area.

Robert has drawn his title as a dominant meandering design, echoing the trunk and branches of the tree beneath it. The black frame to the cover draws the eye into the composition.

Covers without artwork

Publishers sometimes go for the stark, classical, words-only cover design because they want a verbally assertive image. I find that when children are starting out on book art, their covers tend to contain words only. Teachers must often intervene by discussing published book covers to show pupils how they can incorporate narrative picture-making into the design. Robert's *The Ninja*, sub-titled 'A Story Book', shows that he is already learning to communicate information about a book's category.

Planning lettering

The weakness of Cathy's title design – found commonly on hand-written posters everywhere – is that letters have not been evenly spaced out in the area provided for them. Starting from the left, 'The' is widely spaced out, the 'Snow' of Snowman has been drawn, and then it suddenly occurs to the designer that there is hardly any space left to complete the word; the brakes are jammed on and the final letter is only just prevented from tumbling into the abyss off the edge of the paper. The simplest way to avoid this is for children to use a centring device.

The mathematics of lettering

To help children plan their lettering, use a vertical centring device. Distribute fairly wide-lined exercise paper. Pupils draw (or crease) a vertical line down the centre. With odd numbered words, the central letter is drawn first on the central line, then the other letters left and right of this (working backwards to the first letter). With even numbered words, the central line represents the position between the two middle letters.

Refining mathematics

However, if equal distance is given to each letter, pupils will find that they have a poorly designed title. This is due to the difference in the width of letters, for example, the letter 'O' takes up more space than 'C', which takes up more space than 'I'. There is no perfect mathematical way of calculating the spaces between letters or between words. An analysis of this page of type will confirm that! The style of lettering chosen is a significant factor in spacing, but it is the designer who decides what is and what is not well spaced lettering.

'Letters are quantities, and spaces are quantities, and only the eye can measure them,' wrote Ben Shahn (1964), an artist renowned for the inclusion of words in his paintings and engravings. He compared the spaces between letters as akin to the shaping of silence in poetry – invisible, yet as real as the sounds of words themselves.

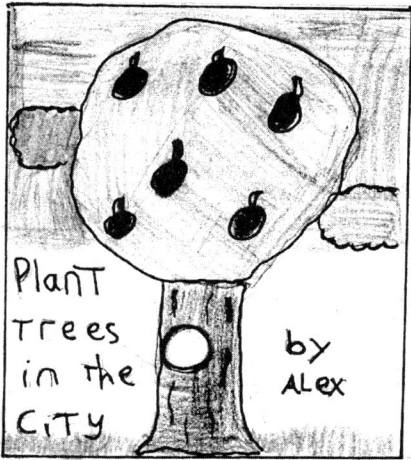

Plant Trees in the City
Alex (aged 7)

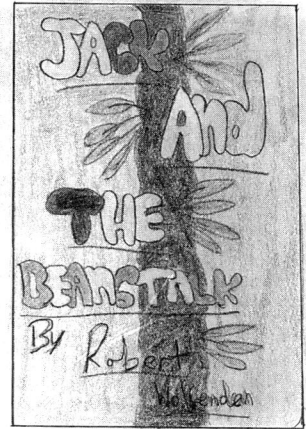

Jack and the Beanstalk
Robert (aged 9)

The Ninja
Robert (aged 9)

Vertical centring

The Snowman
Cathy (aged 8)

Intermingling styles

Because children may still be coming to terms with alphabets, they tend to mix upper case (capitals) and lower case letters in titles; but laziness or a conscious attempt to 'play' with lettering are also factors. They have not far to look to find examples of intentionally mixed alphabets in the advertising media!

Six episodes in the making of a cover design

Mark and Joel worked together on a series of books about the adventures of Superman. It fell to Joel to design the cover for one of them. He made five drafts and a final version:

1   Joel was given an A5 sheet of paper and without guidance asked to design the book's cover. He was advised that it should contain the title and the authors' names.

Observations: *Lettering is placed too far to the left and fails to assert itself.*

2   It was suggested to him that the cover should include an illustration.

Observations: *The title is now placed more centrally, but the authors' names are visually insignificant at the bottom of the cover. The high-rise building emphasises the space in which Superman is placed, but lettering and images are undistinctive.*

3   Joel was given an A5 template to draw around and shown the letter-centring technique. Light horizontal 'tramline' pencil lines were drawn for him where the lettering was to be placed, and a central point, from which letters and spaces were to be arranged, was marked.

Observations: *He gets the SUPE of the title right but then falters with the rest of the spacing, forgetting to keep to the tramlines. The template frame has helped him to see the cover as a*

specific field. *This has resulted in better placed lettering and an assertive single image illustration.*

4   The tramlines are redrawn, top and bottom, and Joel has a second try at placing the lettering accurately.

Observations: *This attempt is more successful although the letterforms at the bottom still falter.*

5   Joel was introduced to outlined lettering design and encouraged to sketch roughly in pencil and finish in pen.

Observations: *His command of drawing letters is improving and all letters are reasonably well shaped and placed. In this and the previous two attempts the central figure has remained unaltered.*

6   This final design shows Joel's developing self-assurance in planning a cover that exploits a range of techniques to arouse attention – dramatic letterforms appropriate to the theme, unconventional ways of presenting lettering, strong visual imagery.

Observation: *All six stages took just under two hours to complete.*

Super Man V
Joel (aged 7)
▶

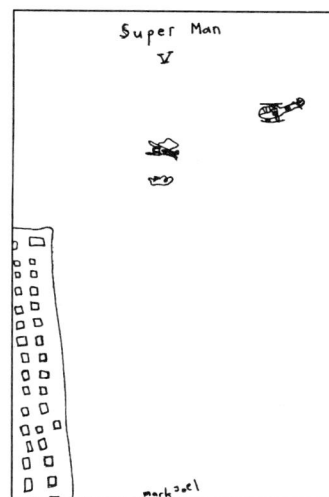

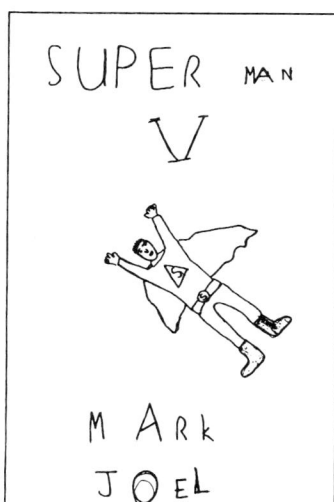

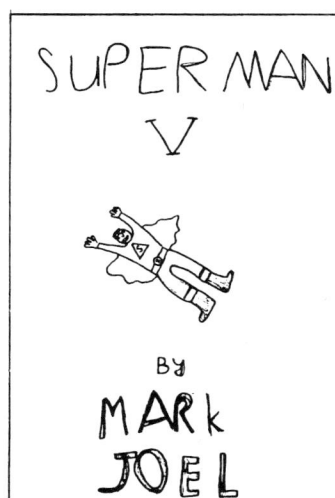

Styles of lettering

Linear and outline letters

Using stencils can seem an ideal solution to the challenge of designing letters, but stencilled lettering rarely looks attractive. Young children can have a very good sense of drawing letters and placing them on their book covers, as Sandra's work shows. Eve's outline letters are confidently well placed. However, this 'natural' feel for design may not flourish, or even survive, if not encouraged and developed.

Roman lettering

Roman lettering is characterised by variations of line thickness and the small tail, the serif, that reaches out from the top and bottom of letterforms. Throughout civilisation, Roman lettering has been identified with all that is sophisticated and stylish. Children learning calligraphy find that the pen can be held in different ways in making these elaborations, but they can also be produced synthetically and used as ornaments to letters.

Neil is acquiring skill at drawing lettering and Rosalyn, using a less formal style, has centred her title reasonably well. The serifs give that extra touch of sharpness and confidence to her lettering.

Optical factors

Correct proportions of letterforms sometimes need to be distorted to compensate for illusory effects:

● When drawing letters of varying thicknesses, make the curved parts of letters wider than the vertical or horizontal parts.
● Make diagonal lines narrow slightly as they converge.
● Curved and pointed letters should extend slightly beyond their guide lines.
● The centre bars of B, E, F and H need to be placed just above the half way point; otherwise they will look too low on the letter.

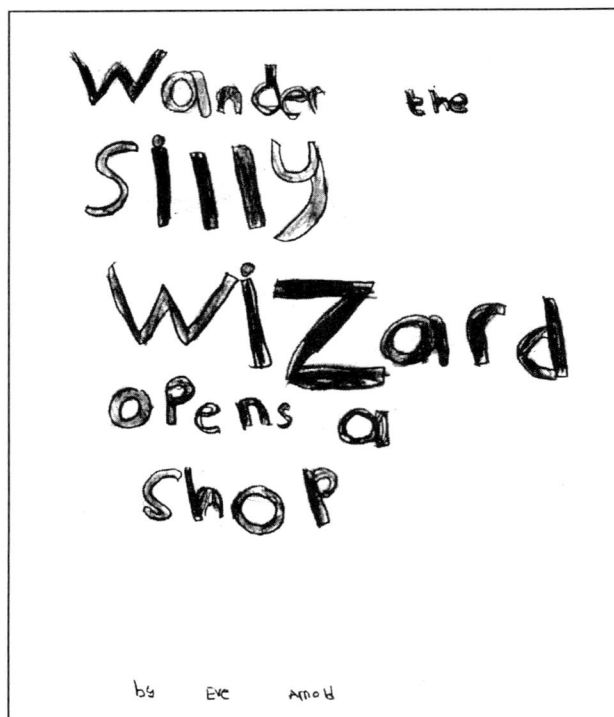

Wander the Silly Wizard Opens a Shop
Eve (aged 5)

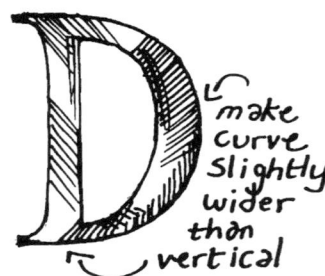

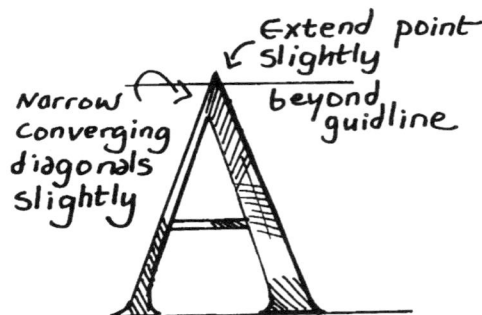

Designed distortion

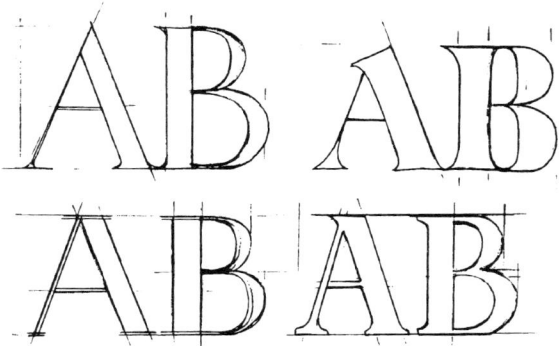

Variations of Roman-style lettering

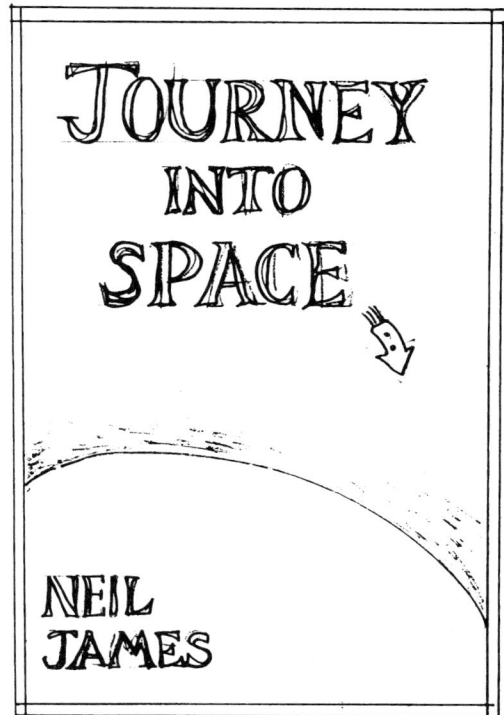

Journey into Space Neil (aged 11)

Bears go Swimming Sandra (aged 6)

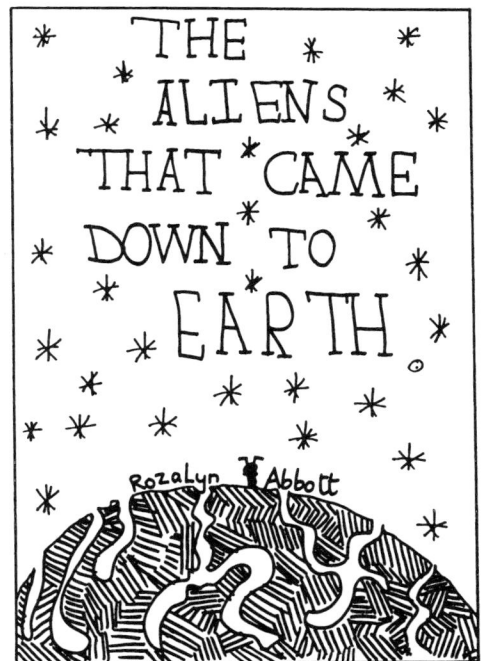

The Aliens that Came Down to Earth
Rosalyn (aged 10)

Playful lettering

Sarah has seen faces in nearly all the 'bubble' letters of her decorative title page. Using figurative forms as letter shapes goes a long way back in book design. Nineteenth-century designers were very fond of it, sometimes to a ridiculous extent, so that the letters themselves disappeared in the artwork undergrowth. This is the problem with using pictorial objects to construct letters – the identity of the letter must not be submerged under the artistic assertion of the forms.

Kurtis uses a similar lettering strategy – shaping the forms to reflect the theme. His letters are drawn rock-like, a play on the title.

Variations of design

Ben's mix of upper and lower cases and styles in his title came from a chalkboard demonstration of different ways of drawing letters. This works well, especially with the sharply defined artwork image made by a monoprinting technique. Lettering which appears to be falling off the page succeeds in this instance because it follows a logical linear pattern.

In Joanne's lively design the first few words of the narrative start at the bottom of the cover. It is an enticing and original way to lure the reader into turning the page and reading away.

My Family Sarah (aged 5)

Rock and Roll Troll Kurtis (aged 9)

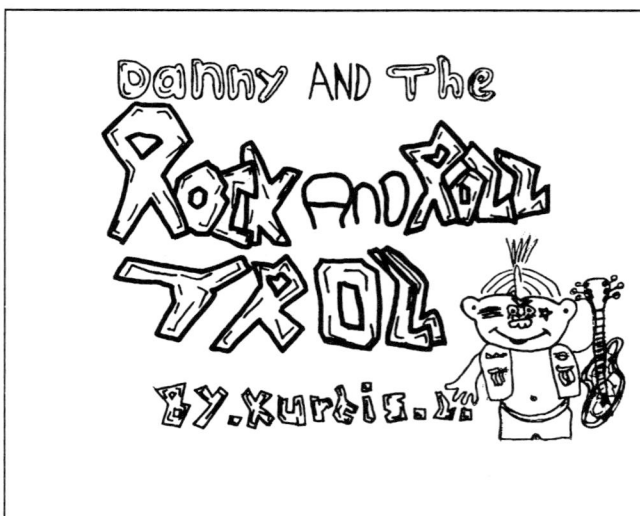

Letterform experiments
made by a primary
school teacher

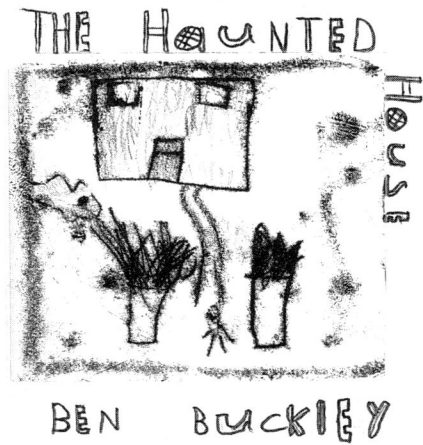

The Haunted House Ben (aged 8)

It was the night before Easter......

The Easter Bunny Joanne (aged 9)

Back cover copy

'This story is about a boy called John', is a typical synopsis to be found on the back covers of children's own books. 'Sara Hunt is 6 years old and likes swimming' is characteristic of an autobiographical outline. If young authors are undirected, their back pages tend, like Simon's, to be influenced by films and THE END appears to state the obvious.

Subordinate to the front cover, the back cover is the secondary window on the book as a whole. This space is usually divided into synopsis, autobiographical details, publisher's 'blurb', publisher's logo, price and bar code. Publication details of a book and details about the publisher (the colophon) usually appear in the pages before the text begins (the 'prelims'). In the basic eight-page concertina book this copy is reserved for the page before the front cover (page 8) – in effect the back 'cover'. (In the basic origami book this copy is actually on the back cover.)

These forms of composition require the writer to think categorically. A one-sentence description of the story demands a mode of thought different from that needed in carefully selecting five words which will 'sell' the book in the publisher's blurb. In basic books, the average page size of which is relatively small, copy has to be minimal.

There is something rather smug and self-congratulatory about back cover copy. It always says wonderful things about the author and indulges in hyperbolic praise of the book itself. Reading out to children this kind of thing from published books, I always say to them, 'Say nice things about your book, like the things these people say about the book I am holding. You've worked as hard on your books as these published authors have on theirs. You deserve it!'

The Plane that Could not Fly Simon (aged 6)

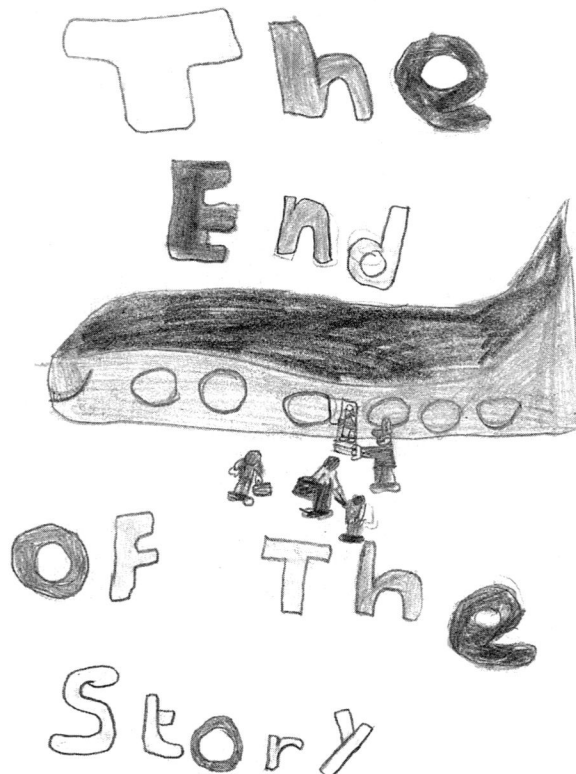

Back cover copy designs
by children aged 5–10

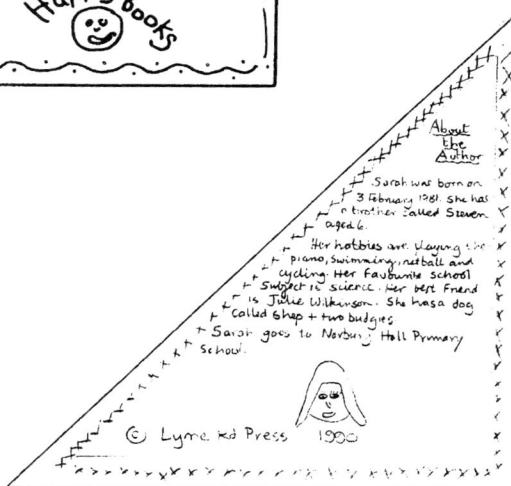

I like
S wimming
Muh

60p

Christmas is going well at Santa's workshop
until Twinkle, Santa's head elf realises
that no toys have been made for African
children. Can Santa and his elves make
some toys and deliver them by Christmas
day?
A Save the children product.

Save   Also thanks to   UK £2.99
the   N.S.P.C.C.   CAN $5.99
Children   AUS $4.80

97801 403

This book is about a fat and a
thin robber.

SWA

The author of this book is
Hayeln Payne who is 10 year Old.
His hobbies are plane spotting
and nature.

An excellent read.
                    The times

My book
Lisa
?P

This book is about
a dog called Rob.

I hope you like it.

Happy books

About
the
Author
Sarah was born on
3 February 1981. She has
a brother called Steven
aged 6.
Her hobbies are playing the
piano, swimming, netball and
cycling. Her favourite school
subject is science. Her best friend
is Julie Wilkinson. She has a dog
called Shep + two budgies.
Sarah goes to Norbury Hall Primary
school.

© Lyne Kid Press 1900

Conclusion

I have tried to design this book so that teachers who are not art specialists can identify some of the basic concepts of graphic design and see how they influence that most essential of classroom tasks – writing. Assessing children's success and failure in graphic design has been encouraged by building this book around examples of their work, reflecting common patterns of behaviour. 'Correct' procedures and techniques have been identified; where and how mistakes are made have been discussed; and ways of improving them have been suggested. Only by the teacher acquiring this 'visual intelligence' can pupils be coached into improving standards in their own work.

In places I have suggested whole-class approaches to organising tasks (for example, by providing a narrative structure for children to slot their ideas into), but as work progresses beyond these preliminary and introductory stages, pupils need the freedom to develop their own individual ways of addressing the task in hand. Throughout this book we have seen that children evolve their own solutions to placing words and pictures on the page. Some of these ideas have come from classroom workshops and suggestions made by teachers, others from immersion in picture books. In some cases it's hard to say how the child has evolved them – perhaps there is a visual intuition in all of us waiting to be realised. So, while providing structured inputs, the teacher must also stand back and let the child's inner sensitivity – with all its weaknesses and faults — have its turn.

At various stages in the book-producing process – for example, designing the cover – it will be appropriate to turn to whole-class teaching, and workshops in brainstorming plots, handwriting, making illustrations and many other areas will become relevant as work progresses. There are, of course, numerous ways in which collaborative strategies can be employed, such as pupils working in pairs or a group of children working on the different aspects of the book and, on completion, assembling them into the final artefact.

How much time is given to the book-art approach to writing will vary from teacher to teacher and the range of curriculum subjects they feel can best be served by it. Bearing in mind that the book arts embrace key curriculum areas like English, art and design technology, it is important to acknowledge that a range of essential skills is addressed in the one 'product'. Not all of these areas will necessarily be addressed equally in one book-making project. Different aspects will be emphasised at the expense of others, but over a school year (or preferably a longer period) the 'body' of skills required for book-art projects can be covered, even if in an elementary form.

More significant than any set of educational justifications, teachers, I hope, will want to pursue the design concepts described in this book because, pragmatically, they will witness how they contribute specifically to the raising of standards in writing, and generally to children's attitudes to learning. The sense of achievement on a child's face at having completed a book successfully should be the starting point for him or her moving up to a new level of accomplishment – eventually, perhaps, as a professional communicator and, in all cases and therefore more importantly, as a creatively fulfilled adult.

Appendix I

Basic book forms

The basic eight page book

CONCERTINA BOOK

① Place paper in front of you (Landscape) & crease vertically in half...

② crease left & right edges to centre...

③ Open, and crease horizontally in half...

④ From these 8 rectangles over 40 books are possible! The simplest are the CONCERTINA & the ORIGAMI

⑤ Fold horizontally in half...

⑥ Crease sections back & forth to make concertina book.

ORIGAMI BOOK

① crease paper to stage 4 of concertina book...

② crease in half vertically and cut half way on folded edge with scissors to make slot through centre creases...

③ slot here

④ Fold on landscape horizontal... push left & right edges to centre

⑤ wrap around any two sections to make 6 page origami book.

EXTENDED CONCERTINA BOOK

① crease 1cm margin on right edge of Landscape...

② crease left edge to margin and crease again to make four pages + 1cm crease....

③ Glue margin to next section. Using this method a concertina book of any length can be produced.

Landscape

Portrait

ORIGAMI BOOK PROCESS

① MAKE BOOK

Draw around template in drafting book

② PREPARE TEXT

what kind of design layouts do you want your book to have?

DRAFT 2

OR Design book on computer and paste up print outs.

③ WRITE BOOK

storyboard

Word list

Draw around template on page

2 3   4 5   6 7

④ ILLUSTRATE BOOK

Do you want decorative borders?

Sketch Book

2 3   4 5

Draw illustrations directly into book or prepare on pieces of paper and glue into book

6 7

⑤ COVERS

FRONT

TYPES OF LETTERING
A B
C

HOLIDAY

A DARK ARMY

JOHN JONES

Plan title on spare paper

BACK

plan back cover copy...

BASIC BOOK LAYOUT PLANS

Appendix 2

Suggested Picture Book Reading

The following list of books can be used to demonstrate some of the aspects of page design discussed in this book.

Formal page layout designs

Mick Inkpen *(1995) Nothing*. London: Hodder Headline.
Full-page text with facing full-page illustrations. By using wide borders the short textual episodes and illustrations are held tightly into the centre of the pages.

Trish Cooke (1994) *So Much* (Illustrated by Helen Oxenbury). London: Walker Books.
Beautifully designed book employing page of text followed by page of illustration but conceived as an informal design.

Tony Ross (1994) *I want to be*. London: Picture Lions.
Tony Ross has produced several picture books like this one in which the single line narrative runs like a caption at the bottom of the page of illustrations.

Less formal page layout designs

Margeret Olivia Wolfson (1996) *Marriage of the Rain Goddess* (Illustrated by Clifford Alexandra Parms). Bristol: Barefoot Books.
In this landscape oriented book, the illustrations fill the whole of the left-side page and cross over to fill half the right-hand page. The remaining half of the page holds the narrative.

Informal page layout designs

Colin McNaughton (1993) *Making Friends with Frankenstein*. London: Walker Books.
As with most of McNaughton's books, every page has an inventively different layout. He integrates cameo cartoon-strip imagery with black and white linework and full colour pictures, speech in bubbles with variations in size of letters and artwork borders. A riot of design resourcefulness.

Babette Cole (1996) *Dr Dog*. London: Red Fox.
Hilarious picture story book with freely arranged text on full page 'bled' illustrations from one of our most humorous writers and illustrators.

Robert Westall (1995) *The Witness* (Illustrated by Sophy Williams). London: Macmillan.
The text is arranged in mounted panels which are inserted into the full-page illustrations.

Border designs

Anthony Browne (1995) *Willy the Wizard*. London: Random House.
Some of the illustrations have no borders, others have thin or thick line borders, and others are coloured and decorated. One border even fades out to nothing! A good example of several different kinds of border design all of which relate to the mood of the page they are on.

Jenny Koralek (1994) *The Boy in the Cloth of Creams* (Illustrated by James Hayhew). London: Walker Books.
A book with irregular pattern border decorations based on the theme of the book.

Meighan Morrison (1995) *Linda Lou*. London: Ashton Scholastic.
A picture book made entirely from fabric collage. Page borders are made from sewn strips of printed cotton.

Children's picture book satire

Jon Scieszka and Lane Smith (1993) *The Stinky Cheese Man and other Fairly Stupid Tales.* London: Picture Puffins.
This book mocks the design of children's picture books. Some pages of type are up-side-down, others disappear off the bottom of the page. The jumbled-up contents page is placed several pages after the story begins, and so it goes on. Not only an outrageous read, but an excellent 'how-not-to-design-your-book' book!

And for other more practical reading...

Tony Potter (1987, reprinted 1993) *Lettering and Design.* London: Usborne Publishing.
This primer on basic book design is as good an introduction as you'll find.

References

Allsburg, C. Van (1985) *The Polar Express.* London: Anderson.

Andersen, H. C. (1913) *Fairy Tales.* London: Hodder and Stoughton (pp. 26, 27).

Arnheim, R. (1974) *Art and Visual Perception.* Berkeley: University of California Press (p.l51).

Bicknell, T. and Trotman, F. (1988) *Professional Illustrators – How to write and illustrate children's books.* London: Macdonald Orbis.

Biggs, J. (1977) *Letter-forms and Lettering.* Poole: Blandford (p. 72).

Book Art Project, The (1993) *Book Pack 3 – Introducing illustration to children.* Manchester: Manchester Metropolitan University – The Children's Press.

Book Art Project, The (1994) *Book Box.* Manchester: Manchester Metropolitan University – The Children's Press.

Bowman, P. (1986) (Illustrator) *Amazing Maisy's Family Tree* by Lynn Zirkel. Oxford: Oxford University Press.

Briggs, R. (1978) *The Snowman.* London: Hamish Hamilton.

Clarke, S. (1994) *The Tombs of the Pharaohs.* London: Tango Books.

Dahl, R. (1982) *The BFG.* London: Jonathan Cape.

Fairbank, A. (1949) *A book of Scripts.* Harmondsworth: Penguin.

Foreman, M. (1991) *War Boy.* London: Pavilion Books.

Hamel, C. de (1992) *Scribes and Illuminators.* London: The British Museum Press.

Inkpen, M. (1991) *Billy's Beetle.* London: Hodder Headline.

James, S. (1991) *Dear Greenpeace.* London: Walker Books.

Johnston, E. (1906) *Writing, Illuminating and Lettering.* London: Pitman.

Lawrie, R. (1993) Abridged and visualised realisation of *The Lion, the Witch and the Wardrobe* by C.S. Lewis. London: Harper Collins.

Livingstone, A. and Livingstone, I. (1992) *The Encyclopaedia of Graphic Design and Designers.* London: Thames and Hudson (p.4).

Marcellino, F. (1991) *Puss in Boots.* London: Victor Gollancz.

Marsh, L. (1970) *Alongside the child.* London: A. & C. Black (p.85).

McLean, R. (1980) *Typography.* London: Thames and Hudson (p.174).

Midda, S. (1990) *Sketchbook from Southern France.* London: Sidgwick and Jackson.

Morris, W. (1898) *A note by William Morris on his aims in founding the Kelmscott Press.* Oxford: Kelmscott Press (Reprinted 1969, Irish University Press).

Ormerod, J. (1992) 'The Inevitability of Transformation' in Styles et al. (Eds) *After Alice.* London: Cassell (pp.42–55).

Ormerod, J. (1988) *The Story of Chicken Licken.* London: Walker Books.

Ryder, J. (1993) *Intimate Leaves from a Designer's Notebook.* Newtown: Gwasg Gregynog (p.31).

Sassoon, R. (1990) *Handwriting – the way to teach it.* Cheltenham: Stanley Thornes (p.1).

Sendak, M. (1993) *We are all down in the dumps with Jack and Guy.* London: Harper Collins.

Shahn, B. (1964) *Love and Joy about Letters.* London: Cory, Adams and Mackay (p.48).

Swann, A. (1989) *How to Design Grids.* Oxford: Phaidon.

Tanner, R. (1946) *Lettering for Children.* Leicester: Dryad Press (pp.21–22).

Tschichold, J. (1992) *The Form of the Book.* London: Lund Humphreys.

Walker, S. (1992) *How it looks.* Reading: The Reading and Language Information Centre and the Department of Typography and Graphic Communication, University of Reading (pp.13, 8–15.

West, S. (1990) *Working with Style.* New York: Watson Guptill (p.36).

Wildsmith, B. (1986) *Goat's Trail.* Oxford: Oxford University Press.